# Barbie™ bakes!

## 50+ Fantastic Recipes from Barbie & Her Friends

weldon**owen**

# CONTENTS

Cream Cheese & Jam Mini
Flower Tarts, page 50

Granola Bars with
White Chocolate Drizzle, page 44

Strawberry-Citrus
Muffins, page 111

# Hey friends!

Anyone who knows me knows why I love baking so much: it's the perfect mix of chemistry and creativity. There's nothing like whipping up a batter, watching it take shape in the oven, and then using your imagination to decorate. And the best part, of course, is sharing what you make with friends and family.

Baking can seem hard. I get it. But it's all about practice! Everyone has to start somewhere, so work at your own pace and try the easy treats first. My granola bars (page 44) and sugar cookies (page 25) are a great place to begin. As your confidence grows, why not test your skills with something a little more difficult like Magical Mermaid Cupcakes (page 94) or my Birthday Cake Surprise (page 80).

Along the way, try experimenting! When I was learning to bake, as I got comfortable in the kitchen, I started adding my own little twists— a pinch of cinnamon here, a dash of vanilla there—to show off my personal style. Those small experiments turned out to be some of my most successful baking efforts! Sure, things don't always go as planned. Just keep in mind that bumps in the baking road are okay, and that a positive attitude changes everything. Remember, too, that as long as you're willing to put in the work and keep trying, you can do anything!

*— Barbie*

# Barbie's Best Baking Tips

## STAY ORGANIZED

Be prepared! First, read through the recipe from beginning to end. Then, gather the equipment and ingredients you'll need and lay them on a clean work surface around you. Next, prepare any ingredients you can in advance. As you work, always keep your hands and the area clean. As soon as you're done with an ingredient, put it away; when you've finished using a tool, set it aside for washing. And once your creation goes into the oven, don't forget to set a timer!

## PRACTICE KITCHEN SAFETY

If you're comfortable using a knife, ask an adult to help you choose the correct type for the task and then hold it firmly by the handle as you work. When you're not using the knife, place it somewhere safe so it won't fall onto the floor or be grabbed by a younger sibling. If you're working with an electric appliance, keep it unplugged except when in use. To guard against burns, never touch a hot oven or a hot pan without first putting on an oven mitt. And don't forget to give your freshly baked treats time to cool before sampling them!

## ASK FOR HELP IF NEEDED

Always keep an adult nearby to guide or assist you as needed. If you're comfortable using a knife, ask them to choose the correct type, and make sure you place it somewhere safe when you're not using it. If you're working with an electric appliance, have an adult around to operate it, and unplug it when not in use. And never touch a hot oven or pan without putting on an oven mitt—or keep an adult around to handle them. Your loved ones want you to succeed, so don't be afraid to ask for their help! Look for the helping hand on recipes that might require some assistance.

## MAKE HEALTHY CHOICES

Desserts are a yummy "sometimes" food: they're great for special occasions, but you never want too much! It's important to balance your diet with "everyday" foods, too: fruits, vegetables, and other rich sources of vitamins, minerals and nutrients. Look for the healthy tips in this book for serving options and substitutions to help keep your body happy and nourished throughout the day.

# Essential Skills

### FILLING & HOLDING A PASTRY BAG

*1* Fit a pastry bag with the desired tip. If you don't have a pastry bag, use a zip-top or sandwich bag as a substitute.

*2* Put the bag, tip end down, into a tall glass and fold back the open end of the bag over the sides of the glass.

*3* If you're adding different-colored swirls to your meringue or frosting, using a clean, food-safe paintbrush, and working from the tip to the top, paint stripes of your first food coloring on opposite sides of the bag. Rinse the brush, then paint your second color on opposite sides, alternating them with the stripes of the first color.

*4* Using a spoon or rubber spatula, scoop your meringue or frosting into the pastry bag. If you have drawn lines to create colored swirls, be careful not to disturb them. Unfold the cuff, push the contents down toward the tip, and twist the bag closed.

*5* To hold the bag for piping, grasp it at the twist with your dominant hand and near the tip with your other hand.

### BUTTERING & FLOURING A PAN

*1* Put a pat of room-temperature unsalted butter on a small piece of waxed paper, parchment paper, or paper towel and spread the butter over the bottom and sides of the pan, coating the entire surface generously and evenly.

*2* To flour the pan, butter it as directed in Step 1, add about 2 tablespoons flour, and then tilt and shake the pan so the flour coats the buttered surface evenly. Tap out the excess flour.

### MEASURING INGREDIENTS

**To measure most dry ingredients**, dip a dry measuring cup into the ingredient and scoop it up so it overflows the rim. Then, using the back of a butter knife or other straight edge, sweep off the excess. Your ingredient should be level with the rim of the cup. Use the same scoop-and-sweep method when using measuring spoons.

**To measure liquid ingredients**, place a liquid measuring cup on a flat surface. Pour the liquid into the cup until it reaches the correct measuring line, then check the line at eye level to ensure accuracy. If using a measuring spoon, hold the spoon over a small bowl (to capture any overflow) and pour in the liquid until it is full.

# The Dreamhouse Pantry

Not sure what to have on hand? Keep these essential ingredients well stocked so you can bake on a moment's notice.

**Flour:** Although most of the recipes in this book call for all-purpose flour, a handful call for these other types: whole wheat, oat, cake, and buckwheat. Read through the recipe carefully to know which flour you need before you begin!

**Sugar:** Always keep three basic types of sugar on hand: granulated sugar, which is small, white granules that pour easily; powdered sugar (aka confectioners' sugar), which is made by crushing granulated sugar to a powder; and brown sugar, a mix of granulated sugar and molasses that comes in two types, light and dark, and has a slight caramel flavor. Sanding sugar (aka pearl sugar), which is large crystals and comes in lots of different colors, is fun to use for decorating.

**Eggs:** When shopping for eggs to use for recipes in this book, make sure you reach for a carton labeled "large." Medium eggs can result in a dry dough or batter, while extra-large or jumbo eggs will yield a dough or batter that's too wet.

**Baking soda:** Unlike baking powder, baking soda must be combined with an acid ingredient, such as buttermilk, yogurt, sour cream, or citrus juice, to release the carbon dioxide that causes cakes, quick breads, and cookies to rise in the oven. Always make sure to measure baking soda accurately, as too much can give whatever you are making a soapy flavor.

**Baking powder:** This fine white powder is made by combining an alkali, baking soda; an acid, such as cream of tartar; and a base, usually cornstarch. When exposed to moisture, baking powder releases carbon dioxide that creates bubbles in your dough or batter, causing whatever you're baking to rise in a hot oven.

**Butter:** Always use unsalted butter. Baking is a science, so using salted butter can throw off your other measurements and the flavor of what you are making.

**Vanilla extract:** This popular flavoring is made by soaking vanilla beans in an alcohol solution to extract their deep, complex flavor and heavenly aroma. Look for bottles labeled "pure vanilla extract." Products labeled "vanilla essence" are not quite as flavorful.

# Cookies, Brownies & Bars

# Chocolate-Dipped Butter Cookie Triangles

You can experiment with your own toppings just like Barbie would: try crushed dried banana or a sprinkling of flaky sea salt. Or invite your friends over and see what they come up with. After all, it is always better when we come up with ideas together!

**1  MAKE THE DOUGH.** In a medium bowl, mix the flour and salt. In a large bowl, using an electric mixer, beat together the butter and sugar on medium speed until light and fluffy, about 3 minutes. Add the vanilla and beat until well combined. Turn off the mixer and scrape down the sides of the bowl with a rubber spatula. Add the flour mixture and beat on low speed just until well mixed and smooth.

**2  CHILL THE DOUGH.** Using the rubber spatula, scrape the dough out onto a piece of plastic wrap. Cover with the wrap, then use your hands to shape the dough into a thick disk. Refrigerate for 30 minutes.

**3  BAKE THE COOKIES.** Preheat the oven to 350°F. Line 1 rimless cookie sheet with parchment paper. Unwrap the dough and set it on a lightly floured work surface. Using a rolling pin, roll out the dough into a 12-inch square about ¼ inch thick. Using a pastry wheel, trim the edges so they are even. Then, using the pastry wheel and a ruler, cut the dough into nine 4-inch squares. Cut each square in half on the diagonal into 2 triangles. You should have 18 triangles. Transfer the triangles to the prepared pan, spacing them about 1½ inches apart. Bake the cookies until the edges are golden brown, 12 to 14 minutes. Let cool completely on the pan on a wire rack.

**4  DIP IN CHOCOLATE.** Put the chocolate chips and coconut oil into a microwave-safe bowl. Microwave on high power, stirring every 20 seconds, just until almost melted, then stir until smooth. Place the bowl of melted chocolate near the cookies. Put the sprinkles into a small bowl and set it near the cookies. Dip each cooled cookie halfway into the melted chocolate, letting the excess chocolate drip back into the bowl. Carefully place the cookie back on the cookie sheet and sprinkle the chocolate on top. Refrigerate for 10 minutes to set the chocolate before serving.

## Makes about 18 cookies

2 cups all-purpose flour, plus more for dusting

½ teaspoon salt

1 cup unsalted butter, at room temperature

½ cup sugar

2 teaspoons pure vanilla extract

1 bag (12 oz) semisweet or bittersweet chocolate chips (2 cups)

2 tablespoons coconut oil or solid vegetable shortening

Rainbow sprinkles for decorating

# Chocolate Heart Sandwich Cookies

You'll want to underbake these cookies slightly so the filling doesn't squish out the sides of the sandwiches when you bite into them. If they do turn out crunchy, do what Barbie does and improvise! Crush the cookies in a bowl, top with berries, and finish with a dollop of whipped cream.

*1* **MAKE THE DOUGH.** In a medium bowl, mix the flour, cocoa powder, baking powder, baking soda, and salt. In a large bowl, using an electric mixer, beat together the butter, brown sugar, and granulated sugar on medium-high speed until light and fluffy, 2–3 minutes. Reduce the speed to low, add the egg and vanilla, and beat until well combined. Turn off the mixer and scrape down the sides of the bowl with a rubber spatula. Add the flour mixture and beat on low speed just until incorporated. Using the spatula, scrape the dough out onto a piece of plastic wrap. Cover the dough with the wrap, shape into a thick disk, and refrigerate until firm, at least 1 hour or up to overnight.

*2* **CUT OUT THE COOKIES.** Preheat the oven to 350°F. Line 2 cookie sheets with parchment paper. Unwrap the dough and set it on a lightly floured work surface. If the dough is too hard to roll directly from the refrigerator, let it stand at room temperature for a few minutes. Dust a rolling pin with flour and roll out the dough ¼ inch thick. Using a 2-inch-wide heart-shaped cookie cutter, cut out as many cookies as possible. Place the cookies on the prepared pans, spacing them about 1 inch apart. Gather up the dough scraps, press them together, roll out, and cut out more cookies. (If the dough has warmed too much to roll easily, wrap and refrigerate until firm, then try again.)

*3* **BAKE THE COOKIES.** Place 1 cookie sheet into the oven and bake the cookies until firm to the touch, 10–12 minutes. Let cool on the pan on a wire rack for 5 minutes, then transfer the cookies directly to the rack and let cool completely. Repeat with the remaining cookie sheet of cookies.

*Continued on next page*

## Makes about 30 cookies

2¼ cups all-purpose flour, plus more for dusting

⅓ cup unsweetened cocoa powder, sifted

½ teaspoon baking powder

½ teaspoon baking soda

¼ teaspoon salt

¾ cup unsalted butter, at room temperature

1 cup firmly packed light brown sugar

¼ cup granulated sugar

1 large egg

1 teaspoon pure vanilla extract

**4** **MAKE THE FROSTING.** In a bowl, using the electric mixer, beat together the butter and sugar on low speed until combined. Increase the speed to medium-high and beat until light and fluffy, about 3 minutes. Reduce the speed to low, add the vanilla and salt, and beat just until combined. Fit a pastry bag with a small round tip. Put the bag, tip end down, into a tall glass and fold back the open end of the bag over the sides of the glass. Using a rubber spatula, scoop the frosting into the pastry bag. Unfold the cuff, push the frosting down toward the tip, and twist the bag closed.

**5** **ASSEMBLE THE SANDWICH COOKIES.** Turn half of the cookies bottom side up. With your dominant hand holding the bag at the twist and your other hand holding it near the tip, pipe the frosting onto the overturned cookies, piping it almost to the edge of each cookie. Top with the remaining cookies, bottom side down. Roll the sides of the sandwiches in sprinkles and/or sanding sugar, if using, then place on a large platter or rimmed baking sheet. Refrigerate until the filling is firm, about 1 hour. Serve the cookies chilled or at room temperature.

FOR THE FROSTING

1 cup unsalted butter, at room temperature

¾ cup powdered sugar

1½ teaspoons pure vanilla extract, or ¼ cup strained raspberry preserves

Pinch of salt

Assorted pink and white sprinkles and/or a mixture of pink and white sanding sugar for decorating (optional)

**HEALTHY TIP!**
Don't want the sprinkles? Roll the sides in crushed nuts for a delicious protein-packed snack.

# Confetti Cookies

Rainbow sprinkles make every bite of these cookies a celebration, but you can also choose sprinkles to match a holiday: try red and pink for Valentine's Day, orange and black for Halloween, or make up your own holiday and use your favorite colors!

*1* **PREPARE THE PANS.** Preheat the oven to 350°F. Line 2 cookie sheets with parchment paper.

*2* **MAKE THE DOUGH.** In a medium bowl, mix the flour, baking powder, and salt. In a large bowl, using an electric mixer, beat together the butter and granulated sugar on medium speed until light and fluffy, 1–2 minutes. On low speed, add the eggs and vanilla and beat until blended. Turn off the mixer and scrape down the sides of the bowl with a rubber spatula. Add about half of the flour mixture and beat on low speed just until blended. Add the remaining flour mixture and beat just until blended. Turn off the mixer, add the sprinkles, and stir until evenly distributed.

*3* **BAKE THE COOKIES.** Scoop up 1 rounded tablespoon of dough, roll it between your palms into a ball, and set the ball on a prepared pan. Repeat with the remaining dough, spacing the balls about 3 inches apart. Place 1 cookie sheet into the oven and bake the cookies just until the edges are light golden brown, about 13 minutes. Let cool on the pan on a wire rack for 5 minutes, then transfer the cookies directly to the rack and let cool completely. Repeat with the remaining cookie sheet of cookies.

*4* **DECORATE THE COOKIES.** To make the icing, in a small bowl, whisk together the powdered sugar, milk, and vanilla until smooth. Spoon about 1 tablespoon of the icing onto each cookie, letting it drip over the edges a little. Decorate with rainbow sprinkles. Let the icing dry at room temperature until firm, at least 2 hours, before serving.

## Makes about 36 cookies

FOR THE COOKIES

2¾ cups all-purpose flour

1 teaspoon baking powder

¼ teaspoon salt

1 cup unsalted butter, at room temperature

1½ cups granulated sugar

2 large eggs

2 teaspoons pure vanilla extract

2 tablespoons rainbow sprinkles, preferably nonpareils

FOR THE ICING

2½ cups powdered sugar

2 tablespoons plus 2 teaspoons whole milk

2 teaspoons pure vanilla extract

Rainbow sprinkles, preferably nonpareils, for decorating

# Butterscotch, Coconut & Macadamia Nut Cookies

 ASK FOR HELP!

Here, rich butterscotch, mellow coconut, and crunchy macadamia add up to a winning cookie. If you don't like butterscotch, dark chocolate chips or walnuts make a delicious alternative.

**1** **PREPARE THE PAN.** Preheat the oven to 325°F. Line 1 cookie sheet with parchment paper.

**2** **MAKE THE DOUGH.** In a medium bowl, mix the flour, baking powder, baking soda, and salt. In a large bowl, using an electric mixer, beat together the butter, granulated sugar, and brown sugar on medium speed until light and fluffy, about 3 minutes. Reduce the speed to low, add the egg and vanilla and beat until combined, about 1 minute. Turn off the mixer and scrape down the sides of the bowl with a rubber spatula. Add the flour mixture and beat on low speed just until blended. Turn off the mixer and, using the spatula, fold in the coconut, butterscotch chips, and macadamia nuts until evenly distributed.

**3** **BAKE THE COOKIES.** Drop the dough by rounded tablespoons onto the prepared pan, spacing the cookies about 2 inches apart. Bake the cookies until golden brown, 16–18 minutes. Let cool on the pan on a wire rack for 5 minutes, then transfer the cookies directly to the rack and let cool completely.

## Makes about 20 cookies

1⅓ cups all-purpose flour

½ teaspoon baking powder

½ teaspoon baking soda

½ teaspoon kosher salt

½ cup unsalted butter, at room temperature

½ cup granulated sugar

½ cup firmly packed light brown sugar

1 large egg

½ teaspoon pure vanilla extract

1¼ cups sweetened shredded dried coconut

½ cup butterscotch chips

¾ cup macadamia nuts, roughly chopped

**HEALTHY TIP!**
Try these cookies with a side of mango slices. It's the perfect summertime treat!

# Stained-Glass Bubble Cookies

ASK FOR HELP!

You can see right through these near-transparent cookies just as if they were a collection of iridescent bubbles! Make them in a variety of sizes—just as if they were real bubbles—using hard candies in a range of pastel hues.

**1  PREPARE THE PANS.** Preheat the oven to 350°F. Line 2 cookie sheets with parchment paper, then lightly spray the parchment with cooking spray.

**2  CRUSH THE CANDIES.** Separate the candies by color. Put each color into a heavy-duty lock-top plastic bag, press out the air, and seal the bag closed. Lay each bag flat and roll a rolling pin over it to crush the candies.

**3  CUT OUT THE COOKIES.** Unwrap the dough and set it on a lightly floured work surface. Dust the rolling pin with flour and roll out the dough ¼ inch thick. Using a 3-inch round cookie cutter, cut out as many cookies as possible. Transfer the cutouts to the prepared cookie sheets, spacing them about 1 inch apart. Using a smaller round cookie cutter, cut out a "window" from the center of each cutout and carefully lift out the smaller round of dough. Gather up the dough scraps and the smaller rounds, press them together, roll out, and cut out more cookies. (If the dough has warmed too much to roll easily, wrap and refrigerate until firm, then try again.) Refrigerate or freeze the cookie sheets until the cutouts are firm, at least 15 minutes.

**4  BAKE THE COOKIES.** Place 1 cookie sheet into the oven and bake the cookies for 8 minutes. Remove the pan from the oven and carefully fill the window of each cutout with crushed candies, keeping the colors separate or mixing them as you wish. Return the pan to the oven and continue to bake until the edges of the cookies are light golden brown and the candies have melted, 6–8 minutes. Let cool completely on the pan on a wire rack before serving. Repeat with the remaining cookie sheet of cookies.

## Makes about 30 cookies

Nonstick cooking spray

All-purpose flour for dusting

1 bag (7 oz) hard candies in assorted colors

Dough for Shimmery Sugar Cookie Stars (page 25) prepared through Step 2

# Shimmery Sugar Cookie Stars

Dip the cookie cutter into flour before pressing it into the dough so the edges don't stick to the dough. And cut out the cookies as close together as possible to minimize scraps. If you don't have a star-shaped cookie cutter, use the shape you have or use a variety of shapes.

*1* **MAKE THE DOUGH.** In a medium bowl, mix the flour, baking powder, and salt. In a large bowl, using an electric mixer, beat together the butter and sugar on medium-high speed until light and fluffy, 2–3 minutes. On low speed, add the egg and vanilla and beat until well combined. Turn off the mixer and scrape down the sides of the bowl with a rubber spatula. Add the flour mixture in three batches, beating on low speed after each addition until the flour is almost fully incorporated. Turn off the mixer and scrape down the sides of the bowl again. Add the cream and beat on low speed just until combined.

*2* **CHILL THE DOUGH.** Using the rubber spatula, scrape the dough out onto a piece of plastic wrap. Cover the dough with the wrap, shape it into a thick disk, and refrigerate until firm, at least 1 hour or up to overnight.

*3* **CUT OUT THE COOKIES.** Preheat the oven to 350°F. Line 2 cookie sheets with parchment paper. Unwrap the dough and set it on a lightly floured work surface. If the dough is too hard to roll directly from the refrigerator, let it stand at room temperature for a few minutes. Dust a rolling pin with flour and roll out the dough ¼ inch thick. If the dough starts to crumble as you roll, use your hands to shape it into a ball, flatten it into a thick disk, and try rolling it out again. Using a 3-inch star-shaped cookie cutter (or star-shaped cutters in different sizes), and dipping it into flour before each cut, cut out as many cookies as possible. Transfer the cutouts to the prepared pans, spacing them about 1 inch apart. Gather up the dough scraps, press them together, roll out, and cut out more cookies. (If the dough has warmed too much to roll easily, wrap and refrigerate until firm, then try again.)

*Continued on next page*

## Makes about 30 cookies

3 cups all-purpose flour, plus more for dusting

1 teaspoon baking powder

½ teaspoon salt

1 cup unsalted butter, at room temperature

1¼ cups sugar

1 large egg

2 teaspoons pure vanilla extract

1 tablespoon heavy cream

Vanilla Cookie Icing (page 116)

Rainbow sprinkles, sanding sugar, and/or other decorations of choice

**HEALTHY TIP!**
Try raspberry jam in place of the vanilla icing to give these stars a tangy tartness.

**4** **BAKE THE COOKIES.** Place 1 cookie sheet into the oven and bake the cookies just until the edges, not the centers, are light golden brown, 14–16 minutes. Let cool on the pan on a wire rack for 5 minutes, then transfer the cookies directly to the rack and let cool completely. Repeat with the remaining cookie sheet of cookies.

**5** **ICE THE COOKIES.** Using icing and sprinkles or other decorations—and your creativity!—decorate the cookies. Let the icing dry at room temperature until firm, at least 6 hours or up to overnight, before serving.

# Dipped Crispy Rice Pops

Not an experienced baker like Barbie? That's okay! Crisp rice cereal treats are a sweet everyone can master! Made into pops, then dipped into pastel-hued melted candy and colorful sprinkles, your favorite bake sale treat gets an easy makeover!

1 **MAKE THE CRISPED RICE CEREAL TREATS.** Place a large piece of waxed paper on a work surface and butter the paper. In a saucepan over low heat, melt the butter. Add the marshmallows and stir until completely melted. Add the cereal and stir until evenly coated. Remove from heat and let cool slightly, then dump the cereal mixture onto the buttered waxed paper. Moisten your hands with water and spread the mixture into a rectangle about 10 x 15 inches. Let cool.

2 **MAKE THE POPS.** Using a long knife, cut the cereal block into rectangles about 2 x 3 inches. Insert a wooden ice pop stick halfway into each rectangle, leaving the other half sticking out to use for holding. You should have about 25 pops.

3 **MELT THE CANDY MELTS.** Pour water to a depth of about 1 inch into a small saucepan and bring to a gentle simmer over medium-low heat. Put the candy melts into a heatproof bowl that will rest on the rim of the saucepan. Place the bowl on the saucepan over (not touching) the simmering water. Heat the candy, stirring often, just until melted and smooth, 5–7 minutes. Remove the pan from the heat. Leave the bowl atop the pan to keep it warm.

4 **DIP AND DECORATE THE POPS.** Pour the sprinkles into a small bowl. Line 2 rimmed baking sheets with waxed paper. Carefully dip and swirl each pop in the melted candy and then dip into the sprinkles. Return the pops to the prepared pans. Refrigerate for 10 minutes to set the coating before serving.

## Makes about 25 pops

3 tablespoons unsalted butter, plus room-temperature butter for the waxed paper

4 cups miniature marshmallows

6 cups crisp rice cereal

1 bag (12 oz) pale pink, yellow, or blue candy melts (2 cups)

Sprinkles for decorating

**HEALTHY TIP!**
A slathering of peanut butter and a topping of crushed nuts and sliced bananas add protein and fiber for a nutritious treat!

# Sprinkle Party Cookie Cups

Like a spray of confetti, each one of these festive cookies feels like a celebration. Use rainbow sprinkles in the cookie dough, then again to decorate the frosting on top.

1. **MAKE THE DOUGH.** In a large bowl, using an electric mixer, beat together the flour, sugar, and salt on low speed just until mixed. Working in three or four batches, sprinkle the butter and cream cheese over the flour mixture and beat on low speed until the dough looks crumbly, about 2 minutes total. Beat in the vanilla. Add the sprinkles and beat just until evenly distributed.

2. **FILL THE MUFFIN CUPS.** Spray the cups of two 24-cup mini muffin pans lightly with cooking spray. Scoop up 1 tablespoon of the dough, roll it into a ball, and then gently press it into a disk about 2 inches in diameter. Press the disk into a prepared muffin cup, gently pressing the dough down into the cup and up the sides to the rim. Repeat to use all of the dough; you should have about 36 cups. Refrigerate the pans until the dough is very cold, at least 1 hour or up to overnight.

3. **BAKE THE COOKIE CUPS.** Preheat the oven to 375°F. Bake the cookie cups until lightly golden and cooked through, 15–18 minutes. Let cool in the pans on a wire rack until cool enough to handle, at least 15 minutes. Gently remove the cookie cups (a butter knife will help ease them out) and place on a serving tray or platter. Let cool completely.

4. **PIPE THE FROSTING.** Make the frosting as directed. Fit a pastry bag with a medium star tip. Put the bag, tip end down, into a tall glass and fold back the open end of the bag over the sides of the glass. Scoop the frosting into the pastry bag. Unfold the cuff, push the frosting down toward the tip, and twist the bag closed. With your dominant hand holding the bag at the twist and your other hand holding it near the tip, pipe a swirl of frosting into each cookie cup. Top the frosting with sprinkles and serve.

## Makes 36 cookies

FOR THE COOKIES

2 cups all-purpose flour

¾ cup granulated sugar

¼ teaspoon salt

¾ cup unsalted butter, at cool room temperature, cut into small pieces

3 tablespoons cream cheese, at room temperature, cut into small pieces

2 teaspoons pure vanilla extract

¼ cup rainbow sprinkles, plus more for topping

Nonstick cooking spray

Sprinkle Cookie Frosting (Page 117)

**HEALTHY TIP!**
Omit the frosting and fill the cups with your favorite berries or yogurt instead.

# Summer Sunset Pavlovas

These gluten-free meringues, named after the Russian ballerina Anna Pavlova, have a crisp crust and a soft, chewy interior, making them a perfect backdrop for the antioxidant-rich berries. Although this recipe is best in summer when berries are abundant, you can bake the meringues any time of the year and top them with your favorite fruit of the season.

1 **PREPARE THE PAN.** Preheat the oven to 325°F. Line a rimmed baking sheet with parchment paper.

2 **MAKE THE MERINGUE.** In large bowl, using an electric mixer, beat together the egg whites and salt on high speed until firm, about 1 minute. Gradually add the sugar, a spoonful or two at a time, and continue to beat until the whites hold stiff, glossy peaks. Sprinkle the cornstarch and vinegar over the whites and fold in gently with a rubber spatula.

3 **SHAPE THE MERINGUE(S).** Spoon 6–8 dollops of the meringue onto the prepared pan, dividing the mixture evenly and spacing them 1–2 inches apart. Or to make 1 large meringue, spoon the meringue into a single large mound. Use the back of the spoon to create an indentation in the center of each mound.

4 **BAKE THE MERINGUE(S).** Bake for 2 minutes, then reduce the oven temperature to 250°F. Continue to bake until crisp to the touch, about 1 hour for individual meringues or 1 hour 40 minutes for a large meringue. Turn off the oven and leave the meringue(s) in the oven to cool completely, about 2 hours or up to overnight. Transfer the meringue(s) to a serving plate. Top with the berries and orange and garnish with the pomegranate seeds and mint, arranging them all attractively. Serve immediately.

## Makes 6–8 servings

4 large egg whites

Pinch of kosher salt

1 cup superfine sugar

1 teaspoon cornstarch

½ white wine vinegar

2 cups mixed fresh berries, such as blueberries, raspberries, and blackberries

1 orange, peeled and cut crosswise into slices

¼ cup pomegranate seeds

Fresh mint leaves for garnish

# Unicorn Kiss Cookies

These cookies with a silly name are seriously scrumptious. They're created when balls of sugar cookie dough are rolled in pastel-hued sanding sugars before baking. White chocolate kisses add a smooch of creaminess to the sugar-coated bites.

1 **PREPARE THE PANS.** Preheat the oven to 350°F. Line 2 cookie sheets with parchment paper.

2 **MAKE THE DOUGH.** In a medium bowl, mix the flour, baking powder, and salt. In a large bowl, using an electric mixer, beat together the butter and sugar on medium speed until blended, about 1 minute. Reduce the speed to low, add the eggs and vanilla, and beat until combined, about 1 minute. Turn off the mixer and scrape down the sides of the bowl with a rubber spatula. Add about half of the flour mixture and beat on low speed just until blended. Add the remaining flour mixture and again beat just until blended.

3 **SHAPE THE COOKIES.** In a shallow bowl, make separate piles of the colored sugars. Scoop up 1 rounded tablespoon of the dough. Scrape the dough off the spoon into your hand and roll between your palms into a ball. Roll a different section of the dough ball in each colored sugar to create a tie-dye effect. Place the ball on a prepared pan. Repeat with the remaining dough, spacing the balls about 3 inches apart on the pans.

4 **BAKE THE COOKIES.** Place 1 cookie sheet into the oven and bake the cookies until the edges are lightly browned but the tops are barely colored, 10–12 minutes. Let cool on the pan on a wire rack for 5 minutes, then transfer the cookies directly to the rack. Repeat with the remaining cookie sheet of cookies.

5 **DECORATE THE COOKIES.** Meanwhile, unwrap the chocolate candies. After the cookies have cooled for 10 minutes, press a candy into the center of each cookie. Let cool completely before serving.

## Makes 36 cookies

2¼ cups all-purpose flour

1 teaspoon baking powder

¼ teaspoon salt

1 cup unsalted butter, at room temperature

1½ cups sugar

2 large eggs

2 teaspoons pure vanilla extract

3–5 sanding sugars in different colors (blue, green, pink, yellow and/or red) for decorating

1 package (10½–12 oz) chocolate candies or kisses

# Pinwheel Cookie Lollipops

ASK FOR HELP!

These two-tone cookie pops are easier to make than you might think! Simply stack two layers of dough in different colors, roll into a log, then slice into cookie spirals. Use the two colors here or any of your favorite hues.

1  **MAKE THE DOUGH.** Preheat the oven to 350°F. Lightly butter a rimmed baking sheet. In a large bowl, using an electric mixer, beat together the butter, sugar, and vanilla on low speed just until blended. Raise the speed to medium-high and beat until creamy and pale in color, about 2 minutes. Turn off the mixer and scrape down the sides of the bowl. Add the flour and beat on low speed until smooth.

2  **TINT AND ROLL OUT THE DOUGH.** Turn out the dough onto a lightly floured work surface and gather it into a ball. Divide the ball in half. Put each half into a small bowl. Add about 15 drops of yellow food coloring to one half of the dough and 15 drops of green food coloring to the other half. Using a fork, mix the coloring into each dough half until evenly blended. Place each dough half on a separate large piece of waxed paper. Using a rolling pin, roll out each half into a 4 x 8-inch rectangle. Pick up the waxed paper holding the green dough and carefully flip the dough rectangle over onto the yellow dough, lining up the edges as evenly as possible, then peel off the waxed paper. Using your hands, press down firmly to seal the layers together. Slowly peel off the top layer of waxed paper.

3  **CUT THE DOUGH.** If needed, using a small knife, trim the edges so they match up evenly. Beginning at a short side of the dough stack, carefully lift and curl the edge of the dough over. Then, using the waxed paper as an aid, roll up the dough layers into a tight log, peeling away the paper as you go. Press the seam to seal and, if needed, trim the ends so they are even. Using a large knife, cut the dough log in half crosswise, then cut each half into 6 equal slices, each about ⅓ inch thick. Place the slices on the prepared pan, spacing them well apart. Gently push a wooden ice pop stick about 1 inch deep into the edge of each slice.

4  **BAKE THE COOKIES.** Bake until lightly golden on the bottoms, 10–12 minutes. Let cool on the pan for a few minutes, then move the cookies directly to the rack and let cool completely before serving.

## Makes 12 cookies

¾ cup unsalted butter, at room temperature, plus more for the pan

¾ cup powdered sugar

1 teaspoon pure vanilla extract

1½ cups all-purpose flour, plus more for dusting

Yellow and green food coloring

# Peanut Butter Sandwich Cookies

Oat flour and buckwheat flour take the place of all-purpose flour in these gluten-free treats. Skip the chocolate filling, if you like, for a simpler and lighter option, or swap it out for a fruit butter, such as blueberry or strawberry.

1 **MAKE THE DOUGH.** In a medium bowl, mix the oat and buckwheat flours, baking powder, baking soda, and salt. In a large bowl, using an electric mixer, beat the butter and granulated and brown sugars on medium-high speed until light and fluffy, about 3 minutes. Add the eggs one at a time, beating well after each addition. Beat in the vanilla and peanut butter. Stop the mixer and scrape down the sides of the bowl with a rubber spatula. On low speed, add the flour mixture and beat just until combined. Cover the bowl and refrigerate until the dough is firm enough to scoop, about 2 hours.

2 **BAKE THE COOKIES.** Preheat the oven to 350°F. Line 2 cookie sheets with parchment paper. Using a small spoon, scoop balls of dough onto the prepared baking sheets, spacing the balls about 2 inches apart. Place 1 cookie sheet into the oven and bake the cookies until the edges are golden brown, 8–10 minutes. Let cool on the pan on a wire rack for 5 minutes, then transfer the cookies directly to the racks and let cool completely. Repeat with the remaining cookie sheet of cookies.

3 **ASSEMBLE THE SANDWICH COOKIES.** Turn half of the cookies bottom side up. Using a spoon, spread a heaping teaspoon of the filling onto each cookie. Top with the remaining cookies, bottom side down, and serve.

## Makes 24 cookies

FOR THE COOKIES

1 cup oat flour

⅓ cup buckwheat flour

½ teaspoon baking powder

½ teaspoon baking soda

½ teaspoon salt

½ cup unsalted butter, at room temperature

½ cup granulated sugar

½ cup firmly packed light brown sugar

2 large eggs

1 teaspoon pure vanilla extract

1 cup creamy peanut butter

Sugar-Free Peanut Butter Chocolate Spread (page 116)

# Yellow & Pink Swirly Meringues

These gluten-free, light-as-air meringues have vibrant hues of pink and yellow, but you can use any of your favorite colors. Use gel paste food coloring, rather than the liquid variety, to paint stripes on the inside of your piping bag for the swirled effect.

*1* **PREPARE THE PAN.** Line a rimmed baking sheet with parchment paper. Lightly spray the parchment with cooking spray.

*2* **MAKE THE MERINGUE.** In a large bowl, using an electric mixer, beat the egg whites on medium-high speed until foamy, about 1 minute. Add the salt and beat until the whites have formed a dense foam, about 1 minute. While beating continuously on medium-high speed, gradually add the sifted sugar, about 2 tablespoons at a time, and continue to beat until the meringue is glossy and very fluffy, about 15 minutes. Add the vanilla and beat just until combined, about 1 minute.

*3* **FILL A PASTRY BAG.** Fit a large disposable pastry bag with a ½-inch star tip. Put the bag, tip end down, into a tall glass and fold back the open end of the bag over the sides of the glass. Using a clean, food-safe paintbrush, and working from the tip to the top, paint 2 stripes of yellow food coloring on opposites sides of the bag. Quickly rinse the brush. Now paint 2 stripes of pink food coloring on opposite sides of the bag and alternating with the yellow stripes. Using a rubber spatula, carefully scoop the meringue into the pastry bag, trying not to disturb the lines of food coloring. Unfold the cuff, push the meringue down toward the tip, and twist the bag closed.

*4* **PIPE THE MERINGUES.** With your dominant hand holding the bag at the twist and your other hand holding it near the tip, pipe the meringue onto the prepared pan, creating mounds 2 inches in diameter and about 1 inch apart. Let the meringues stand at room temperature, uncovered, for 30 minutes. Preheat the oven to 250°F.

*5* **BAKE THE MERINGUES.** Bake the meringues until firm and dry to the touch, 25–30 minutes. If they still feel tacky, turn off the oven and leave them in the oven until completely dry. Let cool completely on the pan on a wire rack, then carefully peel them off the parchment.

## Makes about 24 cookies

Nonstick cooking spray

2 large egg whites, at room temperature

½ teaspoon salt

1 cup powdered sugar, sifted

1 teaspoon pure vanilla extract

Yellow and pink gel paste food coloring

# Tangy Lemon Bars

Silky smooth and tart, lemon bars are delicate but still pack a punch of citrusy flavor. If you don't like the tartness of regular supermarket lemons—Lisbon or Eureka variety—use the juice of Meyer lemons and omit the zest. The result will be a sweeter bar.

*1* **PREPARE THE PAN.** Preheat the oven to 325°F. Press a 20-inch piece of aluminum foil lengthwise onto the bottom and over the short sides of a 9 x 13-inch baking pan. Butter the foil.

*2* **MAKE THE CRUST.** In a large bowl, using an electric mixer, beat together the flour, powdered sugar, lemon zest, and salt on low speed just until blended, about 1 minute. Scatter the butter pieces over the top and beat on low speed until the largest pieces are about the size of peas, about 2 minutes. Turn the dough into the prepared pan and firmly and evenly press it onto the bottom and l inch up the sides. Bake just until the edges are lightly browned, about 20 minutes. Transfer to a rack. Reduce the oven temperature to 300°F.

*3* **MAKE THE FILLING.** In a large bowl, whisk the eggs just until blended. Add the granulated sugar and lemon juice and zest and whisk until smooth, about 1 minute. Sift the flour into the bowl and whisk until incorporated. Slowly pour the filling over the crust. Bake until the filling looks set and does not wobble when the pan is shaken, 40–45 minutes. Let cool in the pan on a wire rack, then cover the pan with plastic wrap and refrigerate until firm, at least 4 hours.

*4* **CUT AND DUST THE BARS.** Holding the edges of the aluminum foil like handles, lift the bar out of the pan and set on a cutting board. Remove the foil. Using a large, sharp knife, cut into 48 small bars. Using a small, fine-mesh sieve, sift the powdered sugar evenly over the tops of the bars before serving.

## Makes 48 bars

FOR THE CRUST

¾ cup cold unsalted butter, cut into ½-inch pieces, plus room-temperature butter for the pan

1½ cups all-purpose flour

½ cup powdered sugar

1½ teaspoons grated lemon zest

¼ teaspoon salt

FOR THE FILLING

6 large eggs

2½ cups granulated sugar

¾ cup fresh lemon juice

1 tablespoon grated lemon zest

½ cup all-purpose flour

2 tablespoons powdered sugar, for dusting

**HEALTHY TIP!**
These lemony bars will go well with your favorite sliced fruit for a wholesome snack.

# Best-Ever Brownies

This is a go-to recipe for chocolate fans. It delivers a double dose of chocolate—dense brownie on the inside and a peanut butter chocolate spread on top. Make a batch before friends come over and you're sure to satisfy everyone's chocolate cravings.

1   **PREPARE THE PAN.** Preheat the oven to 325°F. Lightly butter the bottom and sides of a 9 x 13-inch baking pan. Line the bottom and the two long sides of the pan with parchment paper, allowing it to extend past the rim by about 2 inches on both long sides. Butter the parchment.

2   **MELT THE CHOCOLATE.** To make the brownies, in a large microwave-safe bowl, combine the butter and chocolate. Microwave on high power, stirring every 20 seconds, just until the mixture is almost melted, then stir until smooth. Let cool slightly.

3   **BAKE THE BROWNIES.** In a small bowl, whisk together the flour and salt. Add the eggs to the warm chocolate mixture and whisk until well blended. Add the granulated sugar and vanilla and whisk until the sugar dissolves and the mixture is smooth. Add the flour mixture and whisk just until no white streaks are visible. Pour the batter into the prepared pan and bake until a toothpick inserted into the center comes out with moist crumbs attached, 30–35 minutes. Let cool completely in the pan on a wire rack.

4   **FROST THE BROWNIES.** Holding the edges of the parchment paper like handles, lift the brownie out of the pan and set on a cutting board. Remove the parchment. Using an icing spatula, slather the spread evenly on top. Using a large knife, cut into 16 brownies and serve.

## Makes 16 brownies

FOR THE BROWNIES

¾ cup unsalted butter, at room temperature, plus more for the pan

5 oz unsweetened chocolate, chopped

1 cup all-purpose flour

¼ teaspoon salt

4 large eggs

2 cups granulated sugar

1 teaspoon pure vanilla extract

Sugar-Free Peanut Butter Chocolate Spread (page 116)

# Frosted Cookie Bars

ASK FOR HELP!

When Barbie plans a getaway in her super-stylish DreamCamper, she is always thinking about what treats to take along. Soft, chewy, and topped with fluffy pink frosting, these bars are a great choice for packing up to share with friends on a road trip. Can't get away? They'll brighten a backyard campout, too. Forgo the frosting in favor of jam or fruit preserves.

*1* **PREPARE THE PAN.** Preheat the oven to 350°F. Lightly butter the bottom and sides of a 9 x 13-inch baking pan. Line the bottom and the two long sides of the pan with parchment paper, allowing it to extend past the rim by about 2 inches on both long sides. Butter the parchment.

*2* **MAKE THE DOUGH.** In a medium bowl, mix the flour and salt. In a large bowl, using an electric mixer, beat together the butter and cream cheese on medium speed until well mixed and smooth, about 1 minute. Add the granulated sugar and beat until smooth, about 1 minute. On low speed, add the egg and vanilla and beat until well blended. Turn off the mixer and scrape down the sides of the bowl with a rubber spatula. Add the flour mixture and beat on low speed just until incorporated.

*3* **BAKE THE BARS.** Using the spatula, scrape the dough into the prepared pan and spread it in an even layer. Bake until the edges are light brown, about 30 minutes. Let cool completely in the pan on a wire rack.

*4* **MAKE THE FROSTING.** In a bowl, using the electric mixer, beat the butter on medium speed until creamy, about 1 minute. On low speed, add the powdered sugar, 1 cup at a time, beating after each addition until well mixed. Turn off the mixer and scrape down the sides of the bowl with the spatula. Add the vanilla, blood orange juice, and salt and beat on medium speed until light and fluffy, about 2 minutes.

*5* **FROST AND CUT THE BARS.** Holding the edges of the parchment paper like handles, lift the bar out of the pan and set on a cutting board. Remove the parchment. Using an icing spatula, spread the frosting evenly on top. Decorate with sprinkles, then cut into about 20 bars and serve.

## Makes about 20 bars

FOR THE BARS

1 cup unsalted butter, at room temperature, plus more for the pan

2¾ cups all-purpose flour

½ teaspoon salt

1 package (8 oz) cream cheese, at room temperature

1½ cups granulated sugar

1 large egg

2 teaspoons pure vanilla extract

FOR THE FROSTING

¾ cup unsalted butter, at room temperature

4 cups powdered sugar

2 teaspoons pure vanilla extract

¼ cup fresh blood orange juice, or ¼ cup whole milk mixed with a few dabs red gel paste food coloring

Pinch of salt

Sanding sugar, jimmies, or other sprinkles for decorating

# Soft Strawberry Oatmeal Bars

Strawberry jam is always a favorite—especially homemade—but you can trade it out for any flavor you like. Fruit butters and spreads will make for a slightly less sweet variation.

*1* **PREPARE THE PAN.** Preheat the oven to 350°F. Lightly butter the bottom and sides of a 9 x 13-inch baking pan. Line the bottom and the two long sides of the pan with parchment paper, allowing it to extend past the rim by about 2 inches on both long sides. Butter the parchment.

*2* **MAKE THE DOUGH.** In a food processor, combine the all-purpose flour, whole-wheat flour, sugar, cinnamon, baking soda, salt, vanilla, lemon zest, butter, and water. Pulse a few times until the mixture starts to come together and stick along the sides of the bowl. (Add an additional 1 tablespoon water if the dough is not coming together.) Add the oats and pulse a few times until the oats are chopped and distributed evenly throughout the dough, stopping to scrape down the sides of the bowl with a rubber spatula if needed.

*3* **ASSEMBLE THE BARS.** Using your hands, press half of the dough into the bottom of the prepared pan. (Pressing it will help it stick together.) Check the edges and corners to be sure they are flat and even with the rest of the dough. Using an icing spatula or a butter knife, spread the jam on top of the dough, leaving a ½-inch border around the edge. Pour the remaining dough evenly over the jam layer. Press down lightly with your hands to spread it evenly and help it come together.

*4* **BAKE THE BARS.** Bake until the top is golden brown and the jam bubbles, 30–35 minutes. Let cool completely in the pan on a wire rack. Holding the edges of the parchment paper like handles, lift the bar out of the pan and set on a cutting board. Remove the parchment. Cut into 12 bars.

## Makes 12 bars

¾ cup cold unsalted butter, cut into cubes, plus more for the pan

1 cup all-purpose flour

⅔ cup whole-wheat flour

¾ cup firmly packed light brown sugar

1 teaspoon ground cinnamon

¼ teaspoon baking soda

½ teaspoon salt

2 teaspoons pure vanilla extract

Grated zest of 1 lemon (about 2 teaspoons)

1 tablespoon water

1⅔ cups old-fashioned rolled oats

1½ cups strawberry jam

# Gluten-Free Super Energy Bars

ASK FOR HELP!

Supercharge your day Barbie-style with these gluten-free bites! Pack them to go and you'll be ready for anything, from a robotics competition to a rock concert to just hanging out with friends. They get a little crunch from the crispy rice cereal and yummy sweetness from a mixture of honey, dates, and dried fruit.

1 **PREPARE THE PAN.** Preheat the oven to 350°F. Lightly spray the bottom and sides of a 9-inch square baking pan with cooking spray, then line the bottom and two opposite sides with parchment paper, allowing it to extend past the rim by about 2 inches on both sides. Spray the parchment.

2 **MAKE THE GRANOLA MIXTURE.** In a large bowl, combine the oats, rice cereal, blueberries, salt, and cinnamon. In a food processor, combine the dates, honey, almond butter, and oil and process to a smooth purée, about 2 minutes. Add the date mixture to the oat mixture and stir until well combined. You might want to use your clean hands to mix everything—the mixture is really thick!

3 **BAKE THE BARS.** Scoop and scrape the granola mixture out into the prepared pan and press it firmly onto the bottom. Use a flat-bottomed glass to help create a well-packed, even layer. Bake until golden brown, about 20 minutes. Let cool in the pan on a wire rack just until cool enough to handle.

4 **CUT THE BARS.** Holding the edges of the parchment paper like handles, lift the bar out of the pan and set on a cutting board. Remove the parchment. Cut in half crosswise, then cut each half into 6 equal bars. Remove the pan from the rack, then set the rack in the pan. Arrange the bars on the rack and let cool completely.

5 **ADD THE CHOCOLATE AND SPRINKLES.** Line 1 rimmed baking sheet with parchment paper. Put the chocolate chips into a microwave-safe bowl and microwave on high power, stirring every 20 seconds, just until almost melted, then stir until smooth. Dip the top of each bar into the melted chocolate, then set, chocolate side up, on the prepared baking sheet. Scatter the crushed nuts over the tops of the bars, if using. Refrigerate for 10 minutes to set the chocolate before serving.

## Makes 12 bars

Nonstick cooking spray

2 cups old-fashioned rolled oats

1 cup gluten-free crisp rice cereal

1/3 cup dried blueberries, cranberries, or raisins

1/2 teaspoon salt

1/2 teaspoon ground cinnamon

1/2 cup packed chopped pitted dates (about 12 dates)

1/4 cup honey

3 tablespoons almond butter or peanut butter

3 tablespoons coconut oil or avocado oil

2/3 cup white chocolate chips

Crushed almonds or peanuts (optional)

**HEALTHY TIP!**
Substitute chopped dried strawberries or dried bananas for the dried blueberries, or mix in a handful of chopped toasted nuts.

# Granola Bars with White Chocolate Drizzle

ASK FOR HELP!

Barbie knows that granola tastes best when it's homemade, so she likes to put together her own favorite mix of grains, nuts, seeds, and dried fruit. Start with this recipe, then make it your own—trade in dried cherries for the cranberries or walnuts for the almonds or cashews.

*1* **TOAST THE NUTS.** Prehead the oven to 350°F. Spread the almonds and cashews in a single layer on a rimmed baking sheet and toast in the oven, stirring occasionally, until fragrant, about 10 minutes.

*2* **MAKE THE GRANOLA MIXTURE.** Spray a 9 x 13-inch baking pan baking pan with cooking spray. In a bowl, combine the nuts, oats, cranberries, wheat germ, pumpkin seeds, sunflower seeds, cinnamon, and salt and stir to combine. In a small saucepan, combine the ½ cup coconut oil, sugar, almond butter, and maple syrup over medium heat, bring to a simmer, and cook for 1 minute, stirring constantly. Pour the almond butter mixture evenly over the oat mixture, stir to combine, and let cool for 5 minutes.

*3* **BAKE THE BARS.** Add the egg whites to the granola mixture and stir well. Press the mixture into the prepared pan, packing it down with a rubber spatula. Bake until golden brown around the edges and no longer sticky to the touch, 20–25 minutes. Cut into 12 bars in the pan, then let cool in the pan on a wire rack for at least 1 hour.

*4* **DRIZZLE WITH CHOCOLATE.** Pour water to a depth of about 1 inch into a small saucepan and bring to a gentle simmer over medium-low heat. Put the chocolate chips and the remaining 1 teaspoon coconut oil into a heatproof bowl that will rest on the rim of the saucepan. Place the bowl on the saucepan over (not touching) the simmering water. Heat the chocolate, stirring often, just until melted and smooth, 5–7 minutes. Remove the pan from the heat. Using a spoon, drizzle the chocolate over the bars. Refrigerate for 10 minutes to set the chocolate before serving.

## Makes about 12 bars

½ cup almonds, coarsely chopped

½ cup cashews, coarsely chopped

Nonstick cooking spray

2½ cups old-fashioned rolled oats

1 cup dried cranberries

½ cup wheat germ

¼ cup pumpkin seeds

¼ cup sunflower seeds

1 teaspoon ground cinnamon

½ teaspoon salt

½ cup plus 1 teaspoon coconut oil

½ cup firmly packed light brown sugar

½ cup almond butter

⅓ cup pure maple syrup

2 large egg whites, lightly beaten until frothy

½ cup white chocolate chips

**HEALTHY TIP!**
Don't want the drizzle? These bars also go great with vanilla Greek yogurt.

# Pies & Tarts

# Mini S'mores Tarts with Graham Cracker Crust

When the Roberts camp out, they cook their s'mores the traditional way: on a stick over a campfire. This oven-baked riff on that camping classic is their favorite substitute when they stay at home. Be sure to keep an eye on your s'mores tarts when they are under the broiler. The marshmallows can burn quickly.

1 **MAKE THE CRUSTS.** Put the graham crackers in a large locktop plastic bag, press out the air, and seal shut. Using a rolling pin, roll over the crackers until finely crushed. (You should have about 1 cup crumbs.) In a bowl, stir together the graham cracker crumbs, butter, and brown sugar until evenly moistened. Divide the mixture evenly among six 4-inch tart pans with removable bottoms or standard muffin cups. Press evenly onto the bottoms and up the sides to the rim. If using individual tart pans, place them on a rimmed baking sheet. Freeze for 15 minutes. Meanwhile, preheat the oven to 350°F. Bake the crusts until set, about 10 minutes. Let cool completely in the pan(s) on a wire rack

2 **MAKE THE FILLING.** In a small, heatproof bowl, combine the chocolate chips and butter. Pour the cream into a small saucepan, place over medium heat, and warm the cream just until it starts to simmer. Pour the cream over the chocolate chips and butter. Let stand until the chocolate starts to melt, about 3 minutes, then whisk to combine. Whisk in the granulated sugar and salt until fully dissolved.

3 **FILL THE CRUSTS.** Divide the chocolate mixture evenly among the tart crusts, filling them to just below the rim. Cover with plastic wrap and refrigerate for at least 2 hours or up to 2 days.

4 **BROIL THE S'MORES.** Just before serving, preheat the broiler. Top the tarts with the miniature marshmallows, dividing them evenly. Broil until toasted, about 2 minutes. Let cool, then remove the pan sides from the tartlet pans, or carefully remove the tarts from the muffin cups, and serve.

## Makes 6 mini tarts

FOR THE CRUST

9 graham crackers

6 tablespoons unsalted butter, melted and cooled

2 tablespoons firmly packed dark brown sugar

FOR THE FILLING

1 cup milk chocolate chips

2 tablespoons unsalted butter, at room temperature

½ cup heavy cream

1 tablespoon granulated sugar

½ teaspoon kosher salt

1½ cups miniature marshmallows

# Cream Cheese & Jam Mini Flower Tarts

ASK FOR HELP!

These flower-shaped mini tart shells are the perfect base for creamy no-bake cheesecake with a dollop of sweet jam—a pretty tea party treat. You can cut out the dough and line the pan a week in advance and pop the pan into the freezer. Then bake and fill the shells a day ahead of serving, so you're free to play when your friends arrive for your party.

1 **MAKE THE DOUGH.** In a bowl, mix the flour, granulated sugar, and salt. Scatter the butter over the flour mixture. Using a pastry blender or 2 butter knives, cut in the butter until large, coarse crumbs form. Sprinkle the water over the top and, using a fork, stir and toss lightly until the dough comes together in a rough, shaggy mass. If the dough is too crumbly, mix in a little more water, 1 teaspoon at a time. Dump the dough onto a large piece of plastic wrap, cover with the wrap, and shape into a thick disk. Refrigerate for at least 30 minutes or up to overnight.

2 **ROLL OUT THE DOUGH.** Unwrap the dough and place on a lightly floured work surface. Using a rolling pin, roll out the dough into a round about ⅛ inch thick, lifting and rotating the dough a quarter turn after every pass or two and dusting the work surface with flour as needed to prevent sticking.

**Makes 12 mini tarts**

FOR THE DOUGH

1½ cups all-purpose flour, plus more for dusting

1 tablespoon granulated sugar

¼ teaspoon salt

½ cup cold unsalted butter, cut into small cubes

6 tablespoons ice-cold water, plus more if needed

Nonstick cooking spray

**3  CUT THE DOUGH INTO FLOWERS.** Preheat the oven to 375°F. Lightly spray a 24-cup mini muffin pan with cooking spray. Using a 4-inch flower-shaped cookie cutter, cut out as many flowers as possible. Carefully pull the dough scraps away from the cutouts, press them together, roll out, and cut out more flowers. You should have 12 cutouts.

**4  BAKE THE TART SHELLS.** Transfer a flower cutout to a prepared muffin cup, pressing the center down into the bottom of the cup and folding the petals up and over the edge. Repeat with the remaining cutouts, placing them in every other cup so they are not touching. Use a fork to prick the bottom and sides of the dough a few times. Bake until golden brown, about 20 minutes. Let the tart shells cool completely in the pan on a wire rack, then gently remove the shells from the pan.

**5  MAKE THE FILLING.** In a bowl, using an electric mixer, beat together the cream cheese, cream, powdered sugar, lemon juice, and vanilla on low speed until smooth, creamy, and well mixed, about 1 minute. Fit a pastry bag with a medium round tip or snip the corner from a large lock-top plastic bag. Using a spoon, scoop the cream cheese mixture into the pastry bag. Holding the bag over the pan, pipe the cream cheese mixture into each tart shell, then smooth the top with your fingertip. Each tart should be nearly full. Spoon about ½ teaspoon jam on top, gently spreading it to cover the cream cheese mixture. Arrange on a serving plate and serve right away, or refrigerate for up to 1 day before serving.

**FOR THE FILLING**

2 oz cream cheese (4 tablespoons), at room temperature

2 tablespoons heavy cream

1 tablespoon powdered sugar

¼ teaspoon fresh lemon juice

¼ teaspoon pure vanilla extract

2–3 tablespoons favorite jam, such as strawberry or raspberry, or marmalade

# Cinnamon-Apple Puff Pastry Tarts

This is a mash-up of American apple pie and a jam-filled toaster tart. Use whatever sweet-tart baking apple—that's the type that holds its shape in the oven, rather than collapses into applesauce—you like. Granny Smith, Gala, or Honeycrisp is a good choice. Look for puff pastry in the freezer section of the supermarket.

*1* **MAKE THE APPLE FILLING.** Peel the apples, cut them lengthwise into quarters, and cut out the core from each quarter. Cut each quarter lengthwise into ¼-inch-thick slices, then cut the slices crosswise into ¼-inch pieces. In a frying pan over medium heat, melt the butter. Add the apples, lemon juice, and cinnamon and cook, stirring, until the apples are tender-crisp, about 5 minutes. Add the brown sugar and stir until it melts and is well combined, about 30 seconds. Transfer the apple mixture to a bowl and stir in the flour. Let cool completely.

*2* **ROLL OUT THE DOUGH.** Line a rimmed baking sheet with parchment paper. Lightly dust a clean work surface with flour. Unfold a pastry sheet on the floured surface. Using a rolling pin, roll out the sheet into a slightly thinner rectangle. Using a pastry wheel and a ruler, cut into 6 equal squares. Repeat with the second puff pastry sheet. You should have a total of 12 same-size squares.

*3* **ASSEMBLE THE TARTS.** Divide the cooled apple mixture evenly among 6 pastry squares, leaving a ½-inch border around the edge. Brush the edge of each apple-topped square lightly with some of the egg mixture. Top each with a second pastry square, gently pressing out any air pockets. Using fork tines, press the edge of each tart to seal securely. Transfer the tarts to the prepared pan, spacing them about 2 inches apart. Refrigerate for 30 minutes. Meanwhile, preheat the oven to 425°F.

*4* **BAKE THE TARTS.** Brush the top of each tart with the egg mixture. Using the fork, poke the top of each pastry about three times. Bake until golden brown, about 15 minutes. Using a metal spatula, transfer the tarts to a wire rack and let cool completely before serving.

## Makes 6 mini tarts

FOR THE TARTS

1 lb baking apples

1 tablespoon unsalted butter

1 teaspoon fresh lemon juice

Scant ½ teaspoon ground cinnamon

¼ cup firmly packed light brown sugar

1 teaspoon all-purpose flour

1 package (17 oz) frozen puff pastry (2 sheets), thawed according to package directions

1 large egg, beaten with 1 teaspoon water

# Baked Nectarines with Cinnamon Streusel

ASK FOR HELP!

When you don't want to fuss with making pastry for a fruit pie, here's a fruit-centered alternative: halve and bake the fruit with a buttery streusel topping instead! It's a delicious treat, plus you don't need to peel the fruit, which means you'll eat all the good-for-you fiber and vitamins in the skin. If nectarines aren't in season, you can use peaches, plums, or pluots.

1. **PREPARE THE PAN.** Preheat the oven to 400°F. Line a rimmed baking sheet with parchment paper.

2. **PREPARE THE NECTARINES.** Halve and pit the nectarines and arrange the halves, cut side up, on the prepared pan. If necessary, cut a thin slice off the rounded side of each half so the halves sit flat.

3. **MAKE THE STREUSEL.** In a food processor, combine the flour, sugar, cinnamon, and salt and pulse a few times to mix. Scatter the butter pieces over the flour mixture and pulse just until the mixture resembles coarse crumbs. Do not overmix. Transfer to a bowl and stir in the almonds. Using your hands, squeeze the flour-sugar-butter mixture into small handfuls and scatter it evenly over the nectarine halves, pressing on it lightly so it sticks to the fruit.

4. **BAKE THE NECTARINES.** Bake the nectarines until tender when pierced with a small knife and the topping is nicely browned, about 20 minutes. Transfer 2 nectarine halves to each individual plate and serve right away.

## Makes 4 servings

4 firm, ripe nectarines

¼ cup plus 2 tablespoons whole-wheat flour

¼ cup plus 2 tablespoons firmly packed light brown sugar

½ teaspoon ground cinnamon

⅛ teaspoon salt

2 tablespoons cold unsalted butter, cut into small cubes

⅓ cup roasted almonds, chopped

**HEALTHY TIP!**
For a gluten-free variation, replace the all-purpose flour with oat flour. Gluten-free puff pastry may also be found in the freezer section of the supermarket.

# Lemon Tartlets with Glittery Blossoms

ASK FOR HELP!

Make these tangy mini tarts topped with sugared blossoms for a special celebration. Barbie would probably make sugared lavender flowers (the Roberts family loves lavender lemonade!), but feel free to use your favorite edible flower here; just be sure to ask an adult's permission before working with any flower. You'll need to prepare the flowers a day in advance to give them time to dry.

*1* **MAKE THE SUGARED BLOSSOMS.** Gently wash the flowers under slowly running cool water and then set them on paper towels to dry, blotting them lightly with the towels if needed. The flowers must be fully dry before you begin. Line a rimmed baking sheet with parchment paper. In a small bowl, whisk together the egg white and water until foamy. Put the superfine sugar into a separate small bowl. Working with 1 flower at a time and using a small, clean paintbrush, lightly brush the egg white mixture over the front and back of the flower. Then, holding the flower over the sugar bowl, scoop up a little sugar and sprinkle it over the top, coating the flower completely. Set the flower aside on the prepared pan. Repeat with the remaining flowers. Let the flowers dry at room temperature for 12–24 hours until they are stiff and dry to the touch.

*2* **MAKE THE LEMON CURD.** Fill a saucepan about one-third full with water and bring to a gentle simmer over medium-low heat. Put the whole egg, egg yolks, granulated sugar, and lemon juice into a heatproof bowl that will rest snugly on the rim of the saucepan. Place the bowl on the saucepan over (not touching) the simmering water. Cook, stirring constantly with a wooden spoon or silicone spatula, until thickened, about 5 minutes. Remove from the heat, add the butter, and stir until melted and incorporated. Pour the curd through a fine-mesh sieve placed over a bowl, pressing against the curd with the back of the spoon or spatula to force as much through as possible. Cover the bowl with plastic wrap, pressing it directly onto the surface of the curd (to prevent a "skin" from forming), and let cool until tepid. Refrigerate until chilled, about 1 hour, before using.

*3* **FILL THE TART SHELLS.** Line up the tartlet shells on a work surface. Fill each shell with about 1 tablespoon of the lemon curd, then garnish with the sugared blossoms. (Use any remaining lemon curd for another use.) Arrange the tarts on a serving tray and serve at once.

## Makes 12 tartlets

FOR THE SUGARED BLOSSOMS

8–16 pesticide-free edible flowers, such as violet, pansy, culinary lavender, and/or rose petals

1 large egg white

Few drops of water

Superfine sugar for sprinkling

FOR THE LEMON CURD

1 large whole egg

4 large egg yolks

½ cup granulated sugar

⅓ cup fresh lemon juice, strained

2 tablespoons unsalted butter

12 store-bought mini tart shells, each about 1½ inches in diameter

**HEALTHY TIP!**
For a fresh and fruity variation, fill the tart shells with your favorite yogurt and top with blueberries or thinly sliced strawberries.

# Mixed Berry Galette

Galettes, with their flaky, buttery crusts and vibrant fruit fillings, are wildly popular with nearly everyone. Advanced bakers like Barbie will enjoy customizing the filling with different berry combinations, but novice bakers like Skipper will likely want to follow the directions here—at least for their first berry galette.

*1* **PREPARE THE DOUGH.** Preheat the oven to 425°F. Line a rimmed baking sheet with parchment paper. Make the pastry dough and refrigerate as directed. If using store-bought pastry dough, keep refrigerated until needed. If using homemade pastry dough, unwrap the dough disk and place on a lightly floured work surface. Using a rolling pin, roll out the dough into a round 11–12 inches in diameter and about ⅛ inch thick, lifting and rotating the dough about a quarter turn after every few passes and dusting the work surface with flour as needed to prevent sticking. If using store-bought pastry, lay it flat on the floured surface and, if needed, roll out to the same dimensions. Loosely roll the dough onto the rolling pin, then unroll it over the prepared pan.

*2* **MAKE THE GALETTE.** To make the filling, in a bowl, toss together the berries, lemon juice, granulated sugar, and flour, mixing evenly. Spoon the filling onto the dough, leaving a 2-inch border around the edge. Fold the uncovered edge up and over the filling, forming loose pleats. If you want a sugar-coated crust, brush the border with the beaten egg and sprinkle with the turbinado sugar.

*3* **BAKE THE GALETTE.** Bake until the filling is bubbling and the pastry is golden brown, about 25 minutes. Let cool slightly on the pan on a wire rack. Cut into wedges and serve warm, topped with whipped cream.

## Makes 8 servings

½ recipe (1 disk) Double-Crust Flaky Pie Pastry (page 117), or 1 store-bought rolled pie crust for a 9-inch pie, refrigerated

All-purpose flour for dusting

FOR THE FILLING

2 cups fresh blackberries

2 cups fresh blueberries

2 tablespoons fresh lemon juice

¼ cup granulated sugar

3 tablespoons all-purpose flour

1 large egg beaten with 1 teaspoon water (optional)

1 tablespoon turbinado sugar (optional)

Whipped Cream (page 116) for serving

# Plum Mini Puff Pastry Tarts

These plum-filled pastries are ideal for keeping Barbie fully energized to accomplish everything she does: horseback riding, babysitting, studying, and, of course, baking competitions!

**1** **PREPARE THE PAN.** Preheat the oven to 400°F. Line a rimmed baking sheet with parchment paper.

**2** **MAKE THE TARTS.** Lightly dust a clean work surface with flour. Unfold the pastry sheet on the floured surface and press flat, pinching closed any broken seams. Using a pastry wheel and a ruler, cut the pastry sheet into 4 equal squares. Place the squares well apart on the prepared baking sheet. Top each square with an equal amount of the plum slices, arranging the slices attractively and leaving a ½-inch border around the edge. Sprinkle each tart evenly with 1 tablespoon of the sugar.

**3** **BAKE THE TARTS.** Bake the tarts until the fruit is tender and the pastry is golden brown, 15–20 minutes. Serve warm or at room temperature.

## Makes 4 mini tarts

All-purpose flour for dusting

1 sheet (8½ oz) frozen puff pastry, thawed according to package instructions but still very cold

¾ lb plums, halved, pitted, and cut into ½-inch-thick wedges

4 tablespoons sugar

# Cherry Pie Pops

ASK FOR HELP!

These delightful on-the-go pops are great treats to share with friends no matter the occasion: backyard camping, lounging poolside, stargazing—you name it! If you don't like cherries, you can always swap them out for blueberries or blackberries, or use a combination.

1 **MAKE THE DOUGH.** Make the pastry dough and refrigerate as directed. If using store-bought pastry dough, keep refrigerated until needed. Line a rimmed baking sheet with parchment paper. Submerge 8 wooden ice pop sticks in a glass of water.

2 **MAKE THE FILLING.** In a bowl, stir together the cherries, sugar, flour, and lemon juice. Using a fork, crush half of the cherries to release their juices. Set aside.

3 **ROLL OUT THE PASTRY.** Preheat the oven to 375°F. If using homemade pastry dough, unwrap a dough disk and place it on a lightly floured work surface. Using a rolling pin, roll out the dough disk ⅛ inch thick, lifting and rotating the dough about a quarter turn after every few passes and dusting the work surface with flour as needed to prevent sticking. If using store-bought pastry, lay it flat on the floured surface. Using a 3-inch round cookie cutter, cut out as many rounds as possible and refrigerate the cutouts. Reserve the scraps. Roll and cut out the second disk or store-bought pastry the same way and refrigerate the rounds. Gather up all the dough scraps, press them together, roll out, and cut out more rounds. You should have 16 rounds total. Cut a small vent in the center of 8 of the rounds and refrigerate all the rounds until ready to use.

4 **SHAPE THE PIE POPS.** Place 8 uncut rounds on the prepared baking sheet, spacing them well apart. Using a small pastry brush, brush the edge of each round with some of the egg white. Dry the ice pop sticks with a paper towel. Lay a stick on each round, positioning it so a tip rests on the center of the round. Spoon about 2 teaspoons of the cherry mixture onto the center of each round. Cover each round with a vented round to form the pop. Using the tines of a fork, press around the edge of the pop to seal the rounds together. Brush the top of each pop with the egg white, then sprinkle evenly with sugar.

5 **BAKE THE PIE POPS.** Bake until golden and crisp, 18–20 minutes. Transfer to a wire rack to cool. Serve warm or at room temperature.

## Makes 8 pie pops

Double-Crust Flaky Pie Pastry (page 117) or store-bought rolled pie crusts for two 9-inch pies, refrigerated

FOR THE BERRY FILLING

1 cup pitted fresh cherries, chopped

2 tablespoons sugar

1½ teaspoons all-purpose flour

1 teaspoon fresh lemon juice

All-purpose flour for dusting

1 large egg white, lightly beaten

Sugar for sprinkling

**HEALTHY TIP!**
For even baking, cut a little vent in the top pastry of each pop. Go simple and cut a small circle or cross—or try a heart or star!

# Strawberry Icebox Pie

This creamy, dreamy pink pie is as easy as pie to make. After you bake the crust, all you have to do is whip up the filling, pour it into the crust, and then chill the filling until set. Top the pie with fresh strawberries or a scattering of pastel-hued marshmallows before serving.

*1* **MAKE THE CRUST.** Preheat the oven to 350°F. Put the graham crackers in a large lock-top plastic bag, press out the air, and seal shut. Using a rolling pin, roll over the crackers until finely crushed. (You should have about 1½ cup crumbs.) In a bowl, stir together the cracker crumbs, sugar, butter, and salt until blended. Dump the mixture into a 9-inch pie dish. Then press it firmly and evenly onto the bottom and up the sides of the dish to the rim. A flat-bottomed glass is handy for pressing the crumb mixture so it sticks together. Bake until set and golden brown, about 12 minutes. Let cool completely on a wire rack.

*2* **SOFTEN THE GELATIN AND PURÉE THE BERRIES.** To begin the filling, put the water into a small microwave-safe bowl, sprinkle the gelatin evenly over the top, and whisk gently to combine. Set aside. In a food processor, combine the strawberries and lemon juice and purée until smooth. Pour the purée into a fine-mesh sieve set over a bowl. Use a rubber spatula to press the purée through the sieve, then discard the seeds in the sieve.

*3* **BEAT THE CREAM CHEESE MIXTURE.** In a bowl, using an electric mixer, beat together the cream cheese and vanilla on medium-low speed until blended. Turn off the mixer, then sift the powdered sugar over the cream cheese and pour in the cream. Beat on low speed just until the mixture thickens and is fluffy, about 1 minute. Do not overbeat.

*4* **FINISH THE FILLING.** Add ¼ cup of the strawberry purée to the gelatin mixture. Microwave on high just until hot, about 30 seconds, then whisk until the gelatin dissolves. Pour the gelatin mixture into the bowl with the remaining strawberry purée and stir to combine. Pour the strawberry mixture into the cream cheese mixture. Using the spatula, gently fold the two mixtures together until evenly blended.

*5* **CHILL THE PIE.** Pour the filling into the crust and smooth the top with the spatula. Cover with plastic wrap and refrigerate until set and chilled, about 2 hours. Cut into wedges to serve.

## Makes 8 servings

FOR THE CRUST

12 graham crackers

¼ cup granulated sugar

6 tablespoons unsalted butter, melted and cooled

⅛ teaspoon salt

FOR THE FILLING

3 tablespoons water

1 tablespoon (1 package) powdered unflavored gelatin

3 cups hulled and chopped fresh strawberries (about 1¼ lb berries)

1 tablespoon fresh lemon juice

4 oz cream cheese (about ½ cup), at room temperature

2 teaspoons pure vanilla extract

¾ cup powdered sugar

1½ cups heavy cream

# Raspberry-Lemon Mini Pies

To make these "pielets" even more adorable, line the muffin cups with pretty patterned liners, which means these treats will be even cuter when you display them on a platter or transport them to a get-together. Make sure you make them at least a few hours in advance of serving, as they need to chill before you share them with friends.

*1* **MAKE THE CRUST.** Preheat the oven to 350°F. Line 12 standard muffin cups with paper liners. In a small bowl, stir together the cookie crumbs, sugar, and butter until well combined. Divide the crumb mixture evenly among the lined muffin cups (about 1 tablespoon for each cup). Press evenly onto the bottom of each cup. A flat-bottomed glass is handy for pressing the crumb mixture so it sticks together. Bake until set and golden brown, about 8 minutes. Let cool in the pan on a wire rack. Leave the oven on.

*2* **MAKE THE FILLING.** In a blender or food processor, purée the raspberries until smooth. Strain through a fine-mesh sieve into a bowl and discard the seeds. Set the purée aside. In a small bowl, using an electric mixer, beat the egg whites on medium-high speed just until stiff peaks form. In a medium bowl, whisk together the egg yolks, condensed milk, and lemon juice until blended. Using a rubber spatula, gently fold about one-third of the egg whites into the egg yolk mixture to lighten it. Then fold in the remaining egg whites just until no white streaks remain.

*3* **BAKE THE PIES.** Spoon the filling into the crust-lined muffin cups, dividing it evenly and filling each cup almost full. Spoon about ½ teaspoon raspberry purée on top of each muffin cup. Then, using a toothpick, gently draw swirls of the purée through the filling. Bake the pies until just set in the center, 15–17 minutes. Let cool completely in the pan on a wire rack, then refrigerate until cold, at least 2 hours or up to 3 days, before serving. Top each pie with 2 raspberries just before serving.

## Makes 12 mini pies

FOR THE CRUST

¾ cup finely crushed vanilla wafers (3 oz wafers)

2 tablespoons sugar

3 tablespoons unsalted butter, melted and cooled

FOR THE FILLING

⅔ cup fresh raspberries (½ pint)

2 large egg whites

4 large egg yolks

1 can (14 oz) sweetened condensed milk

½ cup fresh lemon juice

24 fresh raspberries for topping

**HEALTHY TIP!**
These mini pies are great topped with fresh raspberries, but you can use any berry you'd like!

# Key Lime Pie with Pretzel Crust

Salty, sweet, and zesty, this Key lime pie comes together in a snap. The small, round Key lime—aka Mexican lime—can be hard to find fresh, so you will probably need to rely on bottled juice for making this recipe.

ASK FOR HELP!

1 **MAKE THE CRUST.** Preheat the oven to 350°F. In a food processor, pulse the pretzels until finely ground. Add the sugar, butter, and salt and pulse until the texture resembles wet sand. Dump the mixture into a 9-inch pie dish, then press it firmly and evenly onto the bottom and up the sides of the dish to the rim. A flat-bottomed glass is handy for pressing the crumb mixture so it sticks together. Bake the crust until golden brown, about 10 minutes. Let cool completely on a wire rack. Leave the oven on.

2 **MAKE THE FILLING AND BAKE THE PIE.** In a large bowl, whisk together the egg yolks until blended. Add the condensed milk and lime zest and juice and whisk to mix well. Pour the filling into the cooled crust. Place the pie dish on a rimmed baking sheet. Bake the pie until the edges are set but the center still jiggles slightly, 18–22 minutes. Let cool completely on the wire rack, then cover and refrigerate for at least 2 hours or up to overnight before serving.

3 **SERVE THE PIE.** Using a spatula, spread the Whipped Cream on top of the chilled pie. Alternatively, scoop the cream into a pastry bag fitted with a medium star tip and pipe the cream decoratively on top. Garnish with the lime, if using, and serve.

## Makes 8–10 servings

FOR THE PRETZEL CRUST

4½ cups pretzels (about 7 oz)

1 tablespoon firmly packed light brown sugar

½ cup unsalted butter, melted and cooled

Pinch of salt

FOR THE FILLING

8 large egg yolks

2 cans (14 oz each) sweetened condensed milk

4 teaspoons grated regular lime zest

1 cup fresh or bottled Key lime juice

Whipped Cream (page 116) for topping

Grated regular lime zest or thin lime slices for garnish (optional)

# Apple-Blueberry Crumble

Crumbles, crisps, cobblers—these homey baked fruit desserts all have one thing in common: the fruit is crowned with a biscuit or streusel topping. Here, a buttery flour-based streusel turns golden brown and crunchy in the oven. Serve this old-fashioned crumble warm with scoops of vanilla ice cream.

**1  PREHEAT THE OVEN.** Preheat the oven to 400°F. Have ready a 2-quart baking dish.

**2  MAKE THE TOPPING.** In a bowl, combine the butter, flour, and salt. Give everything a quick stir with your hands and then, using your fingertips, rub the pieces of butter into the flour. When the mixture looks like bread crumbs, with no big lumps of butter, stir in the superfine sugar with a spoon. Refrigerate the topping while you make the filling.

**3  MAKE THE FILLING.** Cut the apples lengthwise into quarters and cut out the core from each quarter. Cut the quarters into chunks or rough slices. Put the apples and blueberries into the baking dish and sprinkle the granulated sugar and cinnamon over the top. Stir to mix well.

**4  BAKE THE CRUMBLE.** Spoon the topping evenly over the fruit. Bake until the fruit juices are bubbling at the edges and the topping is golden and firm to the touch, about 30 minutes. Let cool for at least a few minutes before serving. Scoop the crumble onto serving plates and serve warm or at room temperature.

## Makes 4 servings

⅔ cup cold unsalted butter, cut into small cubes

1½ cups all-purpose flour

Pinch of salt

½ cup superfine sugar, light brown muscovado sugar, or a mixture

1½ lb firm green apples, such as Granny Smith, Pippin, or a mixture

1⅓ cups fresh blueberries

1 tablespoon granulated sugar

Pinch of ground cinnamon

# Peach-Blackberry Crisp

ASK FOR HELP!

Barbie always tries to be perfect, but she knows that all you can do is do your best. This recipe is great to make if you don't have time to bake a pie or if you want to practice your baking skills. Whatever your goal, don't be afraid to try! Remember, the only sure way to fail is not to try at all.

1 **MAKE THE TOPPING.** Preheat the oven to 375°F. In a small bowl, stir together the oats, sugar, flour, nuts, cinnamon, nutmeg, and salt. Add the butter and, using your fingertips, rub the butter into the oat mixture until well blended and the mixture is crumbly.

2 **LAYER THE FRUIT AND TOPPING.** In a bowl, combine the peaches and berries and stir gently to mix well. Divide the fruit evenly among eight 8-oz gratin dishes, or dump it all into one 9 x 13-inch baking dish. Spread the fruit in an even layer. Scatter the topping evenly over the fruit. If using gratin dishes, arrange them on a rimmed baking sheet.

3 **BAKE THE CRISP.** Bake until the juices are bubbling and the topping is richly browned, 30–35 minutes. Remove from the oven and let cool for at least a few minutes before serving. Serve the crisp in the gratin dishes or scoop the crisp from the baking dish onto individual serving plates. Serve warm or at room temperature, accompanied with a scoop of ice cream, if desired.

## Makes 8 servings

FOR THE TOPPING

½ cup old-fashioned rolled oats

½ cup firmly packed light brown sugar

¼ cup all-purpose flour

¼ cup finely chopped almonds or pecans

½ teaspoon ground cinnamon

¼ teaspoon ground nutmeg

¼ teaspoon salt

6 tablespoons unsalted butter, at room temperature

2 lb peaches (about 6 medium), halved, pitted, peeled, and sliced

1 cup fresh blackberries

Vanilla ice cream for serving (optional)

# Cakes & Cupcakes

# Unicorn Angel Food Cake

A cloud-like confection fit for angels, this classic American cake gets its sky-high stature and light and airy texture from a dozen beaten egg whites. It's good plain or you can dress it up with a dollop of whipped cream and a spoonful of berries.

1. **MAKE THE BATTER.** Sift together the flour and ¾ cup of the sugar into a small bowl. In a large bowl, using an electric mixer, beat together the egg whites, cream of tartar, and salt on medium speed until an opaque and foamy mixture forms, about 1 minute. Increase the speed to medium-high and continue to beat until soft, glossy peaks form, 2–3 minutes. Reduce the speed to medium and add the remaining 1 cup sugar a little at a time. Once all of the sugar is incorporated, continue to beat until stiff peaks form, about 2 minutes. Add the vanilla and almond extracts and beat just until blended. Add the sifted flour-sugar mixture in four batches, gently but quickly folding in each batch with a rubber spatula with as few strokes as possible. Divide the batter evenly among 3 bowls, add a few drops of a different food coloring to each bowl, and fold very gently just until evenly blended

2. **BAKE THE CAKE.** Preheat the oven 325°F. Gently transfer the batter, one color at a time, to a 10-inch angel food cake pan or other 10-inch tube pan, smoothing the top of each layer with the back of a spoon. Bake the cake until the top springs back when lightly touched with your fingertips, about 40 minutes. Alternatively, insert a toothpick near the center. If it comes out dry, the cake is done. If it comes out wet or with crumbs clinging to it, bake for 5 minutes longer and check again.

3. **UNMOLD THE CAKE.** Remove the pan from the oven and invert it onto a heatproof work surface. Let cool until the cake and the pan are cool to the touch, about 1 hour. Turn the pan right side up and run a thin-bladed knife around both the center tube and the outer edge of the pan to loosen the cake sides. Then turn the cake out of the pan onto a serving plate and serve.

## Makes 10–12 servings

1 cup cake flour

1¾ cups sugar

12 large egg whites, at room temperature

1 teaspoon cream of tartar

¼ teaspoon salt

2 teaspoons pure vanilla extract

½ teaspoon pure almond extract

Food coloring in 3 colors of choice

# Sunshine Sparkle Bundt Cake

ASK FOR HELP!

This cake, with its yellow-and-orange swirled interior and sparkly exterior, is an explosion of color. It's an awesome cake to serve at a sleepover or a birthday party: cut the cake and watch your friends' faces light up as the colorful inside is revealed. Go all out and tint the icing yellow and orange, too!

**1  PREPARE THE PAN.** Preheat the oven to 325°F. Butter a 10-inch Bundt pan, then dust with flour, tapping out the excess.

**2  MAKE THE BATTER.** In a medium bowl, mix the flour, baking soda, and salt. In a large bowl, using an electric mixer, beat together the butter and sugar on medium-high speed until light and fluffy, 5–7 minutes. Add the eggs one at a time, beating well after each addition. Add the vanilla and beat until blended. Turn off the mixer and scrape down the sides of the bowl. On low speed, add the flour mixture in three additions alternately with the sour cream in two additions, beating just until blended after each addition.

**3  MARBLE THE BATTER.** Scoop a heaping 1 cup of the batter into a small bowl. Then scoop another heaping 1 cup of the batter into a second small bowl. Pour the remaining batter into the prepared pan, spreading it evenly with a rubber spatula. Add 8 drops of yellow food coloring to the batter in 1 small bowl, and 8 drops of orange food coloring to the batter in the other small bowl. Using the rubber spatula, gently fold the food coloring into each bowl of batter, rinsing the spatula after each use. Spoon blobs of the yellow batter over the plain batter in the pan, then spoon blobs of the orange batter between the yellow blobs. To marble the batter, draw a wooden skewer or chopstick through the batter in a series of figure eights.

**4  BAKE THE CAKE.** Bake the cake until a toothpick inserted near the center comes out clean, 1¼–1½ hours. Let cool in the pan on a wire rack for 10 minutes. Invert the pan onto the rack, lift off the pan, and let the cake cool completely.

**5  ICE THE CAKE.** Using a spoon, drizzle the icing over the cake so it runs down the sides. Scatter the glitter on top. Let stand for about 10 minutes to allow the icing to set, then cut into slices and serve.

## Makes 12–16 servings

1 cup unsalted butter, at room temperature, plus more for the pan

3 cups cake flour, plus more for the pan

¼ teaspoon baking soda

¼ teaspoon salt

2½ cups granulated sugar

6 large eggs, at room temperature

2 teaspoons pure vanilla extract

1 cup sour cream

Yellow and orange food coloring or colors of choice

Vanilla Cake Icing (page 116)

Edible glitter, confetti, or other sprinkles for decorating

**HEALTHY TIP!**
Sliced bananas and a dash of cinnamon make a perfect complement for this sunny treat.

# Chocolate Swirl Cake

ASK FOR HELP!

Two batters—one chocolate, one vanilla—make this cake deliciously marbled on the inside, while the fudgy frosting elevates it to celebration status. When you are swirling the two batters together, make sure you don't swirl them too much or you will end up with a solid brown cake.

1 **MAKE THE BATTER.** In a medium bowl, mix the flour, baking powder, and salt. In a large bowl, using an electric mixer, beat together the butter, 1¾ cups of the sugar, and the vanilla on medium speed until creamy, about 3 minutes. Add the eggs one at a time, beating well after each addition. Turn off the mixer and scrape down the sides of the bowl. On low speed, add the flour mixture in three additions alternately with the milk in two additions, beating just until blended after each addition.

2 **MAKE THE CHOCOLATE BATTER.** Scoop 2 cups of the batter into a medium bowl. In a small bowl, stir together the cocoa powder and hot water until smooth. Stir in the remaining 2 tablespoons sugar and the baking soda until dissolved. Add the cocoa mixture to the 2 cups batter and stir to mix well.

3 **SWIRL THE BATTERS AND BAKE THE CAKE LAYERS.** Preheat the oven to 350°F. Butter two 8-inch round cake pans, then dust with flour, tapping out the excess. Divide the vanilla batter evenly between the prepared pans. Scoop half of the chocolate batter on top of each vanilla layer. Using a small, thin offset spatula, gently draw swirls through the batters to create a marbled effect. Bake the cake layers until a toothpick inserted into the center of each layer comes out clean, 30–35 minutes. Let cool completely in the pans on wire racks, then unmold onto the racks.

4 **FROST THE CAKE AND SERVE.** Using a serrated knife and a sawing motion, trim off the rounded top from each layer so the layers are flat on both sides. Place a cake layer, top side up, on a serving plate. Scoop about one-third of the frosting onto the layer, then, using an offset or icing spatula, spread the frosting evenly on top. Position the second cake layer, top side up, on the first layer and spread the remaining frosting around the sides and on the top of the cake. Cut into wedges and serve.

## Makes 10–12 servings

2¼ cups all-purpose flour, plus more for the pan

1 tablespoon baking powder

¼ teaspoon salt

¾ cup unsalted butter, at room temperature, plus more for the pan

1¾ cups plus 2 tablespoons sugar

2 teaspoons pure vanilla extract

3 large eggs, at room temperature

1⅓ cups whole milk, at room temperature

⅓ cup unsweetened cocoa powder

¼ cup hot water

¼ teaspoon baking soda

Creamy Fudge Frosting (see facing page)

# Creamy Fudge Frosting

ASK FOR HELP!

The chocolate and cream give this frosting a dense, rich flavor, while sifting the powdered sugar into the frosting adds a welcome boost of airiness. Wait until the cake has cooled completely before applying the frosting, as it will melt if it is spread on the warm cake.

*1* **MELT THE CHOCOLATE.** In a heavy saucepan over low heat, combine the butter and cream. Heat, stirring often, until the butter melts. Add the chocolate and whisk gently until melted and smooth, about 2 minutes. Remove from the heat and let cool to lukewarm, about 8 minutes.

*2* **FINISH THE FROSTING.** Transfer the lukewarm chocolate mixture to a bowl, add the sour cream, and whisk until well blended. Scoop the powdered sugar into a sifter. Then, while whisking constantly, gradually sift the sugar into the chocolate mixture, continuing to whisk until no lumps remain.

*3* **COOL THE FROSTING.** Place the bowl in the refrigerator and let the frosting cool and thicken, whisking every 10 minutes, until thick enough to spread, about 30 minutes. (To thicken the frosting faster, place the bowl of frosting in a larger bowl of ice and whisk until thickened.) If the frosting becomes too stiff to spread, rewarm briefly over low heat and whisk again until smooth.

## Makes about 2⅔ cups

4 tablespoons unsalted butter

¼ cup heavy cream

1 package (12 oz) semisweet or bittersweet chocolate chips (2 cups), coarsely chopped

¾ cup sour cream

1¼ cups powdered sugar

**HEALTHY TIP!**
Dark chocolate contains healthy antioxidants. This recipe makes just enough frosting to decorate one double-layer cake.

# Confetti Cake

Colorful sprinkles decorate this cake inside and out, making it a festive treat fit for birthdays and other special occasions. Long, skinny sprinkles, sometimes called jimmies, work better for this cake than round, hard nonpareil sprinkles, which can streak during baking.

1 **PREPARE THE PANS.** Preheat the oven to 325°F. Lightly butter the bottom and sides of three 8-inch round cake pans. Line the bottom of each pan with parchment paper and butter the parchment. Dust the pans with flour, tapping out the excess.

2 **BEGIN THE BATTER.** In a medium bowl, sift together the flour, baking powder, baking soda, and salt. In a large liquid measuring cup, whisk together the whole milk, buttermilk, and water. In a large bowl, using an electric mixer, beat the butter on medium speed until smooth, about 3 minutes. Add the sugar and vanilla and beat until light and fluffy, about 2 minutes. Add the eggs one at a time, beating well after each addition.

3 **FINISH THE BATTER.** On low speed, add the flour mixture to the butter mixture in four batches alternately with the milk mixture in three batches, beating just until well mixed after each addition. Turn off the mixer after each addition and scrape down the sides of the bowl. When the final batch is incorporated, using a rubber spatula, gently fold in 1 cup of the sprinkles.

4 **BAKE THE CAKE LAYERS.** Divide the batter evenly among the prepared pans and smooth the tops with the spatula. Bake the cake layers until a toothpick inserted into the center of each layer comes out clean, about 40 minutes. Let cool in the pans on wire racks for 20 minutes, then invert onto the racks, lift off the pans, and peel off the parchment. Let the cake layers cool completely.

5 **ASSEMBLE THE CAKE.** Using a serrated knife, trim off the rounded top from each layer so the layers are flat on both sides. Place a cake layer, top side up, on a serving plate. Scoop about one-fourth of the frosting onto the layer, then, using an offset or icing spatula, spread the frosting on top. Position a second layer, top side up, on the first layer and spread with another one-fourth of the frosting. Top with the third layer. Frost and decorate the top and sides with the remaining frosting and 1 cup sprinkles, then serve.

## Makes about 10 servings

1 cup unsalted butter, at room temperature, plus more for the pans

3¼ cups all-purpose flour, plus more for the pans

1 tablespoon baking powder

1 teaspoon baking soda

¾ teaspoon salt

¾ cup whole milk

½ cup buttermilk

¾ cup water

1¾ cups sugar

1 tablespoon pure vanilla extract

3 large eggs

2 cups rainbow sprinkles, preferably jimmies

Buttercream Frosting (page 117)

# Cherry Cheesecake

ASK FOR HELP!

This easy cake is fun to make, though you'll need to ask an adult to help you test if it is done. Here's a tip on how to bring cream cheese to room temperature quickly: remove the foil wrapper, put the cream cheese on a microwave-safe plate, and microwave in 15-second bursts, flipping it over after each burst, until soft but not warm.

*1* **MAKE THE CRUST.** In a bowl, stir together the graham cracker crumbs, butter, and sugar until evenly moistened. Dump the mixture into a 9-inch springform pan. Then press it firmly and evenly onto the bottom and 2 inches up the sides of the pan. Refrigerate the crust while you make the filling.

*2* **MAKE THE FILLING.** Preheat the oven to 300°F. In a large bowl, using an electric mixer, beat together the cream cheese, flour, and salt on medium speed until fluffy and smooth, about 3 minutes. Turn off the mixer and scrape down the sides of the bowl. Add the sugar, sour cream, and vanilla and beat on medium-high speed until smooth. Turn off the mixer and scrape down the sides of the bowl again. On medium-high speed, add the eggs one at a time, beating well after each addition.

*3* **BAKE AND CHILL THE CHEESECAKE.** Remove the crust from the refrigerator and pour the filling into it. Bake the cheesecake for 65–70 minutes. To test for doneness, using oven mitts, nudge the pan; the center of the cake should jiggle slightly. Let cool completely in the pan on a wire rack. Cover with plastic wrap and refrigerate until cold (overnight is best).

*4* **TOP WITH CHERRIES.** Loosen the clasp on the pan sides and remove the sides. Slip a wide metal spatula between the crust and the pan bottom and slide the cake onto a serving plate. Arrange the cherry halves on top of the cheesecake. Serve right away.

## Makes 8 servings

FOR THE CRUST

1½ cups finely crushed graham cracker crumbs (about 9 crackers)

½ cup unsalted butter, melted and cooled

3 tablespoons sugar

FOR THE FILLING

4 packages (8 oz each) cream cheese, at room temperature

2 tablespoons all-purpose flour

¼ teaspoon salt

1¼ cups sugar

½ cup sour cream

1 tablespoon pure vanilla extract

3 large eggs

TOPPING

1¼ lb cherries, pitted and halved

# Lemon-Blueberry Drizzle Cake

The blueberries in this moist cake add a soft sweetness that cuts the tanginess of the lemon. Be sure to toss the berries in flour as directed before adding them to the batter. Otherwise, they'll sink to bottom of the pan during baking.

*1* **MAKE THE BATTER.** In a small bowl, sift together 1½ cups of the flour, the baking powder, and salt. In a large bowl, using an electric mixer, beat together the butter, sugar, and lemon zest on medium-high speed until light and fluffy, 2–3 minutes. Add the eggs one at a time, beating well after each addition. Turn off the mixer and scrape down the sides of the bowl. Add the milk and vanilla and stir until blended. Add the flour mixture and stir just until blended. In a small bowl, toss the blueberries with the remaining 1 teaspoon flour. Add to the batter and stir just until evenly mixed.

*2* **BAKE THE CAKE.** Preheat the oven to 375°F. Butter the bottom and sides of a 9 x 5-inch loaf pan, then dust with flour, tapping out the excess. Using a rubber spatula, scrape the batter into the prepared pan and smooth the top. Bake the cake until golden brown and a toothpick inserted into the center comes out clean, about 55 minutes. Let cool in the pan on a wire rack for a few minutes, then invert the pan onto the rack and lift off the pan. Turn the cake onto its side to cool while you make the syrup.

*3* **MAKE THE SYRUP AND BRUSH ON THE CAKE.** In a small saucepan over medium heat, combine the lemon juice and granulated sugar and bring to a simmer, stirring to dissolve the sugar. Simmer until the mixture is syrupy, about 2 minutes. Using a long wooden skewer, pierce the sides and bottom of the warm cake at least 1 inch deep all over. Brush the bottom and sides generously with the syrup. You may not need all of it. Leave the cake on its side to cool completely.

*4* **MAKE THE GLAZE.** In a small bowl, stir together the powdered sugar and lemon juice until smooth. When the cake is completely cool, place it, top side up, on a serving plate and drizzle the glaze over the cake so it drips down the sides. Let stand until the glaze sets, about 10 minutes, before serving.

## Makes 8 servings

FOR THE CAKE

1½ cups plus 1 teaspoon all-purpose flour, plus more for the pan

1 teaspoon baking powder

½ teaspoon salt

½ cup unsalted butter, at room temperature, plus more for the pan

¾ cup granulated sugar

1 tablespoon grated lemon zest

3 large eggs

½ cup whole milk

1 teaspoon pure vanilla extract

1 cup blueberries

FOR THE SYRUP

3 tablespoons fresh lemon juice

3 tablespoons granulated sugar

FOR THE GLAZE

½ cup powdered sugar

1 tablespoon fresh lemon juice

# Barbie's Birthday Cake Surprise

This is the ultimate birthday cake when you want to impress. You'll need two 8-inch round cake pans and one 9-inch round cake pan (or you can use three 9-inch pans). You can also bake all the layers in 9-inch pans and make a standard three-layer cake with frosting between the layers and fondant on the top. For added glamour, cut out flowers, stars, and/or hearts from the extra fondant and put them on the cake.

1  **PREPARE THE PANS.** Preheat the oven to 350°F. Spray the bottom and sides of two 8-inch round cake pans and one 9-inch round cake pan with cooking spray. Line the bottom of each pan with parchment paper.

2  **MAKE THE BATTER.** Sift the cocoa into a small, heatproof bowl. Slowly add the boiling water to the cocoa while whisking constantly to dissolve the cocoa. Let cool completely. In a medium bowl, sift together the flour, baking soda, and salt. In a large bowl, using an electric mixer, beat together the granulated sugar and butter on medium speed until pale and fluffy, about 3 minutes. Add the eggs one at a time, beating well after each addition. Add the vanilla and cocoa mixture and beat until blended. Turn off the mixer and scrape down the sides of the bowl. On low speed, add half of the flour mixture, then the buttermilk, and finally the remaining flour mixture, beating well after each addition. Beat until the batter is smooth, turning off the mixer once or twice to scrape down the sides of the bowl.

3  **BAKE THE CAKE LAYERS.** Divide the batter among the prepared pans, filling each pan to the same level. The 9-inch pan will need a little more batter than the 8-inch pans. Smooth the tops with a rubber spatula. Bake the cake layers until they begin to pull away from the sides of the pans and a toothpick inserted into the center of each layer comes out clean, about 30 minutes. Let cool in the pans on wire racks for 15 minutes, then invert the pans onto the racks, lift off the pans, and peel off the parchment. Using a serrated knife and a sawing motion, trim off the rounded top from each layer so the layers are flat on both sides.

*Continue on next page*

## Makes 10–12 servings

FOR THE CAKE

Nonstick cooking spray

1 cup plus 2 tablespoons unsweetened cocoa powder

1½ cups boiling water

2½ cups all-purpose flour

2¼ teaspoons baking soda

½ teaspoon salt

3 cups granulated sugar

1 cup unsalted butter, at room temperature

5 large eggs

2 teaspoons pure vanilla extract

1¾ cups buttermilk

Buttercream Frosting (page 117)

Pink and yellow food coloring (optional)

24 oz pink rolled fondant

Powdered sugar for dusting

**4** **MAKE THE FROSTING.** Make the frosting as directed. Set aside about ⅔ cup for decorating. Leave the remaining frosting white or add a few drops of pink food coloring and beat until blended.

**5** **CUT THE CAKES.** Choose 2 bowls or round cardboard disks that are staggered in size. One should be slightly smaller than the 9-inch cake layer (6½ to 7 inches), and the other should be slightly smaller than the first bowl or cardboard disk (5 to 5½ inches). Using a small knife and the larger bowl or cardboard round as a guide, cut down one 8-inch layer. Using the smaller bowl or cardboard round, cut down the second 8-inch layer. These cake layers will create your tiers.

**6** **FROST THE CAKES.** Using an offset or icing spatula, frost each cake layer with a medium-thick layer on top and a thin layer around the sides. Refrigerate the frosted layers while you roll out the fondant.

**7** **ROLL OUT THE FONDANT.** Divide the fondant into 3 pieces, staggering them in size: small (6 oz), medium (7½ oz), and large (10½ oz). Place the small piece of fondant on a work surface dusted with powdered sugar. Following the package directions, knead the fondant until pliable then, using a rolling pin, roll out into a thin round (about ⅛ inch). Repeat with the medium and large fondant pieces.

**8** **COVER THE CAKES.** Remove the cake layers from the refrigerator. Working with the smallest fondant round, roll it completely around the rolling pin, position it next to the smallest layer, and slowly unroll the fondant, draping it evenly over the layer. Repeat with the remaining 2 fondant rounds, covering the medium and large layers the same way. Smooth the fondant over the top and sides of each cake layer. Trim around the base, leaving about a ¼-inch overhang, then tuck the overhang under the bottom of the layer.

**9** **STACK AND DECORATE THE CAKE.** Leave the reserved frosting white or add 1–2 drops yellow food coloring and beat until blended. Transfer the largest layer to a cake plate. Top it with the medium layer and then with the small layer. Smooth the edges of the fondant. Fit a pastry bag with a small star tip. Put the bag, tip end down, into a tall glass and fold back the open end of the bag over the sides of the glass. Using a spoon, scoop the reserved frosting into the pastry bag. Unfold the cuff, push the frosting down toward the tip, and twist the bag closed. With your dominant hand holding the bag at the twist and your other hand holding it near the tip, pipe the frosting all along the seams where the cake tiers meet and along the bottom of the large tier. Decorate with additional pieces of fondant, cut into shapes, if you like. Refrigerate until ready to serve.

# Rainbow Cupcakes

These cupcakes are both beautiful and super easy to make. Plus, they are fun to decorate! Once you get the hang of baking, you can be the master baker of your own family like Barbie is of hers and invite siblings or parents to help you decorate.

*1* **MAKE THE BATTER.** In a medium bowl, mix the flour, baking powder, and salt. In a large bowl, using an electric mixer, beat together the butter and sugar on medium-high speed until light and fluffy, 2–3 minutes. Add the whole eggs and egg yolks one at a time, beating well after each addition. Turn off the mixer and scrape down the sides of the bowl. Add the vanilla and beat on medium-high speed until combined. Reduce the speed to low, add about half of the flour mixture, and mix just until blended. Add the sour cream and food coloring and beat just until combined. Add the remaining flour mixture and beat just until blended.

*2* **BAKE THE CUPCAKES.** Preheat the oven to 350°F. Line 24 standard muffin cups with paper or foil liners. Divide the batter evenly among the prepared muffin cups. Bake the cupcakes until the tops are light golden brown and a toothpick inserted into the center of a cupcake comes out clean, 22–24 minutes. Let cool in the pans on wire racks for 10 minutes, then carefully transfer the cupcakes directly to the racks. Let cool completely, about 1 hour.

*3* **DECORATE THE CUPCAKES.** Using an offset or icing spatula, spread the tops of the cupcakes with the frosting. Cut the sour belts in half crosswise. Arc half of a sour belt like a rainbow and insert the ends into the frosting on each cupcake. Arrange marshmallows at the base of each arc to simulate clouds. Arrange the cupcakes on a large platter or tray and serve.

## Makes 24 cupcakes

2¾ cups cake flour

1 tablespoon baking powder

½ teaspoon salt

1 cup unsalted butter, at room temperature

1¾ cups sugar

4 large whole eggs

2 large egg yolks

2 teaspoons pure vanilla extract

1 cup sour cream

8 drops of blue food coloring

Pillowy Cloud Frosting (page 86)

Rainbow sour belts for decorating

Miniature marshmallows for decorating

**HEALTHY TIP!**
Make a fresh fruit sunrise cupcake! Replace the sour belt and marshmallows with a topping of minced pineapple, minced strawberries, and sliced orange segments.

# Pillowy Cloud Frosting

This frosting gets its creamy, fluffy texture in part from the addition of cream of tartar, which helps stabilize the egg whites. Make sure the mixture is warm when you add the marshmallows so they melt fully.

1  **HEAT THE EGG WHITE MIXTURE.** Fill a saucepan about one-third full with water and bring to a simmer over medium heat. Put the egg whites, sugar, water, corn syrup, cream of tartar, and salt into a heatproof bowl that will rest snugly on the rim of the saucepan. Place the bowl on the saucepan over (not touching) the simmering water and heat the mixture, whisking constantly, until the sugar dissolves and the mixture is very warm to the touch (about 160°F on an instant-read thermometer), about 2 minutes. Turn off the heat and carefully remove the bowl from the saucepan.

2  **FINISH THE FROSTING.** Using an electric mixer, beat the egg white mixture on medium-high speed until it holds soft peaks when the beaters are lifted (be sure to turn off the mixer before you lift the beaters) and is still warm, about 2 minutes. Turn off the mixer and add the marshmallows and vanilla. Beat on low speed until the marshmallows are melted and the frosting is completely smooth, about 2 minutes.

## Makes about 5 cups

2 large egg whites

1 cup sugar

6 tablespoons water

1 tablespoon light corn syrup

½ teaspoon cream of tartar

Pinch of salt

1 cup miniature marshmallows

1 teaspoon pure vanilla extract

# Disco Party Cupcakes

ASK FOR HELP!

These happy, colorful cupcakes will turn any get-together into a party! These are pretty big, so if you want them a little smaller, divide the batter among 12 muffin cups instead of 10 cups and reduce the baking time by a few minutes.

*1* **PREPARE THE MUFFIN CUPS.** Preheat the oven to 350°F. Line 10 standard muffin cups with paper liners.

*2* **MAKE THE BATTER.** In a medium bowl, mix together the flour, baking powder, baking soda, and salt. In a large bowl, using an electric mixer, beat together the butter and granulated sugar on medium-high speed until pale and fluffy, about 3 minutes. Beat in the eggs one at a time, beating well after each addition. Add the vanilla and beat until blended. Turn off the mixer and scrape down the sides of the bowl. On low speed, add half the flour mixture and beat just until combined. Add the sour cream and beat just until blended. Add the remaining flour and beat just until combined. Turn off the mixer and scrape down the sides of the bowl. Mix one last time on medium speed until well blended, about 10 seconds.

*3* **TINT THE BATTER.** Divide the batter evenly among 6 small bowls. Add a few drops of a different color of food coloring—red, orange, yellow, green, blue, and purple—to each bowl, stirring it into the batter. You will have 6 different colors of the rainbow. Dollop a heaping teaspoonful of each color into each prepared muffin cup. Make sure each color is evenly distributed among the 10 cups.

*4* **BAKE THE CUPCAKES.** Bake the cupcakes until a toothpick inserted into the center of a cupcake comes out clean, 15–18 minutes. Let cool in the pan on a wire rack for 15 minutes, then carefully transfer the cupcakes to the rack. Let cool completely, about 1¼ hours.

*Continue on next page*

## Makes 10 cupcakes

1½ cups all-purpose flour

1½ teaspoons baking powder

½ teaspoon baking soda

¼ teaspoon salt

½ cup unsalted butter, at cool room temperature

¾ cup granulated sugar

2 large eggs

1 teaspoon pure vanilla extract

½ cup sour cream or plain whole-milk yogurt

Red, orange, yellow, green, blue, and purple food coloring

Buttercream Frosting (page 117)

Sparkling sugar, rainbow sprinkles, and/or edible glitter for decorating

**5** **DECORATE THE CUPCAKES.** Lay a large piece of plastic wrap—about 12 by 16 inches—on a clean work surface. Spoon each colored frosting into a separate lock-top plastic bag, twist the top closed, and cut off a corner. Beginning at a narrow end of the plastic wrap, pipe thick 11-inch-long vertical stripes of each frosting color side by side in rainbow order (red, orange, yellow, green, blue, purple), starting 1-inch in from the edge of the plastic wrap and finishing at the middle of the plastic wrap. Repeat the rainbow stripes, leaving a 1-inch border at the opposite edge, so you have 2 rows of each color. Fold the 1-inch border over the frosting, then roll up the plastic wrap like a jelly roll. Twist one end closed and leave the other end open. Fit a large pastry bag with a medium-large star tip and insert the frosting roll, open end first, into the bag. Push the frosting down toward the tip and twist the top of the bag closed. With your dominant hand holding the bag at the twist and your other hand holding it near the tip, pipe a rainbow swirl of frosting onto each cupcake. Decorate each cupcake with sparkling sugar. Serve right away, or cover and refrigerate for up to 1 day before serving.

# Sparkle Mountain Cupcakes

Be sure to pipe a frosting base to the edge of the cupcake so you can stack the frosting high—like a mountain. The frosting is so rich and chocolaty that you'll want to eat it from the bowl! You can sneak a little spoonful or two but no more, or your "mountains" will be hills.

*1* **MELT THE BUTTER AND CHOCOLATE.** Put the butter and chocolate into a microwave-safe bowl. Microwave on high power, stirring every 20 seconds, just until melted and smooth. Let the mixture cool until barely warm, 10–15 minutes.

*2* **MAKE THE BATTER.** In a medium bowl, mix the flour, cocoa powder, baking powder, and salt. Add the sugar to the chocolate mixture and whisk until combined. Add the eggs one at a time, beating well after each addition. Add the vanilla and whisk until blended. Add the flour mixture and mix just until combined and no traces of flour are visible. Do not overmix.

*3* **BAKE THE CUPCAKES.** Preheat the oven to 350°F. Line 12 standard muffin cups with paper or foil liners. Divide the batter evenly among the prepared muffin cups. Bake the cupcakes until a toothpick inserted into the center of a cupcake comes out with only a few crumbs attached, 22–24 minutes. Let cool in the pan on a wire rack for 10 minutes, then carefully transfer the cupcakes directly to the rack. Let cool completely, about 1 hour.

*4* **FROST THE CUPCAKES.** Fit a pastry bag with a medium star tip. Put the bag, tip end down, into a tall glass and fold back the open end of the bag over the sides of the glass. Using a spoon, scoop the frosting into the pastry bag. Unfold the top of the bag, push the frosting down toward the tip, and twist the bag closed. With your dominant hand holding the bag at the twist and your other hand holding it near the tip, pipe the frosting on top of each cupcake in the shape of a mountain. Put the sprinkles into a small bowl. Finish the top and sides of the "mountain" by carefully and gently rolling them in the sprinkles. Serve right away.

## Makes 12 cupcakes

½ cup plus 3 tablespoons unsalted butter, cut into pieces

3 oz bittersweet chocolate, chopped

⅔ cup all-purpose flour

2½ tablespoons unsweetened cocoa powder, sifted

¾ teaspoon baking powder

¼ teaspoon salt

¾ cup plus 2 tablespoons sugar

3 large eggs

1 teaspoon pure vanilla extract

Chocolate Frosting (page 117)

Colored sprinkles for decorating

# Strawberry Shortcakes

Here's a great idea for a get-together with your friends: a shortcake party! Bake the biscuits before your friends arrive, then set them out on a plate along with bowls of strawberries, whipped cream, and powdered sugar and let your friends put together their own shortcakes.

1 **PREPARE THE PAN.** Preheat the oven to 375°F. Line a rimmed baking sheet with parchment paper.

2 **MAKE THE BISCUIT DOUGH.** In a large bowl, mix the flour, granulated sugar, baking powder, and salt. Scatter the butter over the flour mixture. Using a pastry blender or 2 butter knives, cut in the butter until the mixture looks like coarse crumbs, with some chunks the size of peas. Pour in the cream and toss and stir with a wooden spoon until the dough starts to come together.

3 **SHAPE THE BISCUITS.** Turn out the dough onto a floured work surface and pat it into a thick disk. Using a rolling pin, roll it out into a round about 1 inch thick, dusting the work surface with flour as needed to prevent sticking. Using a 3-inch round biscuit cutter, cut out 4 biscuits. Using a metal spatula, carefully move the cutouts to the prepared pan, spacing them well apart. Gather up the dough scraps, press them together, roll out, and cut out 2 more biscuits. Transfer them to the prepared pan..

4 **BAKE THE BISCUITS.** Bake the biscuits until golden brown on top, 18–20 minutes. Let cool completely on the pan on a wire rack.

## Makes 6 servings

FOR THE BISCUITS

2 cups all-purpose flour

¼ cup granulated sugar

2 teaspoons baking powder

¼ teaspoon salt

6 tablespoons cold unsalted butter, cut into small cubes

¾ cup heavy cream

1 pound strawberries, hulled and quartered

1–2 tablespoons granulated sugar

Whipped Cream (page 116)

Powdered sugar for dusting

**HEALTHY TIP!**
Add some diced mango and toasted coconut flakes for a vitamin-rich dessert!

**5** **PREPARE THE STRAWBERRIES.** While the biscuits are cooling, put the berries into a bowl and sprinkle with the granulated sugar. The amount of sugar you use depends on how sweet the berries are—taste one! Let the berries stand for 10 minutes.

**6** **ASSEMBLE THE SHORTCAKES.** Using a serrated knife, split each cooled biscuit in half horizontally. Place the bottoms, cut side up, on serving plates and spoon the strawberries on top, dividing them evenly. Add a big spoonful of whipped cream and top with the biscuit tops, cut side down. Put the powdered sugar in a fine-mesh sieve, hold it over each shortcake, and tap the side of the sieve to dust the shortcake. Serve right away.

# Magical Mermaid Cupcakes

ASK FOR HELP!

According to Barbie, baking is a perfect science. But sometimes you are faced with the need to improvise. For example, these cupcakes call for buttermilk. If you don't have any on hand, you'll need to create a substitute. See page 118 for conversions and substitutions.

*1* **PREPARE THE MUFFIN CUPS.** Preheat the oven to 375°F. Line 18 standard muffin cups with paper or foil liners.

*2* **MAKE THE BATTER.** In a medium bowl, mix the flour, baking powder, baking soda, and salt. In a large bowl, using an electric mixer, beat together the butter and sugar on medium-high speed until light and fluffy, 2–3 minutes. Add the eggs one at a time, beating well after each addition. Turn off the mixer and scrape down the sides of the bowl. Add the vanilla and beat on medium-high speed until combined. Reduce the speed to low, add about half of the flour mixture, and beat just until blended. Pour in the buttermilk and beat until combined. Add the remaining flour mixture and beat just until blended. Turn off the mixer, scrape down the sides of the bowl, and give the batter a final stir; it will be thick.

*3* **TINT AND MARBLE THE BATTER.** Scoop one-third of the batter into a small bowl. Then scoop another third of the batter into another small bowl. Transfer the remaining third of the batter to the prepared muffin cups, dividing it evenly and smoothing the top. Add 4 dabs of blue food coloring to the batter in 1 small bowl, and 2 dabs each of red and blue food coloring to the batter in the other small bowl. Using a rubber spatula, gently fold the food coloring into each

## Makes 18 cupcakes

2 cups all-purpose flour

2 teaspoons baking powder

½ teaspoon baking soda

½ teaspoon salt

½ cup plus 2 tablespoons unsalted butter, at room temperature

1 cup sugar

2 large eggs

2 teaspoons pure vanilla extract

1⅓ cups buttermilk

Blue and red gel paste food coloring

Buttercream Frosting (page 117)

Mermaid sprinkles, pastel sprinkle mix, or other sprinkles for decorating

bowl of batter, rinsing the spatula well after you mix the first bowl. Spoon the blue batter in blobs over the plain batter in the muffin cups, spacing them evenly apart. Then spoon blobs of the purple batter between the blue batter blobs. To marble the batter, draw a wooden skewer or chopstick through the batter in a series of figure eights, being careful not to overmix.

**4** **BAKE THE CUPCAKES.** Bake the cupcakes until the tops are light golden brown and a toothpick inserted into the center of a cupcake comes out clean, about 17 minutes. Let cool in the pans on wire racks for 10 minutes, then carefully transfer the cupcakes directly to the racks. Let cool completely, about 1 hour.

**5** **TINT THE FROSTING AND DECORATE THE CUPCAKES.** Divide the frosting among 3 small bowls. Add 2 drops of red food coloring to 1 bowl, then mix with a rubber spatula until the frosting is tinted pink. Add 3 dabs of blue food coloring to the second bowl and mix until the frosting is tinted blue. Add 2 dabs of red food coloring and 1 dab of blue food coloring to the third bowl, then mix until the frosting is tinted purple. Fit a pastry bag with a small star tip. Put the bag, tip end down, into a tall glass and fold back the open end of the bag over the sides of the glass. Viewing the pastry bag in thirds, spoon the pink frosting into the bag, keeping it on one side and filling only one-third of the bag. Then spoon the blue frosting into the bag, keeping it to another side and filling only one-third of the bag. Finally, spoon the purple frosting into the remaining one-third of the pastry bag. Unfold the cuff, push the frosting down toward the tip, and twist the bag closed. With your dominant hand holding the bag at the twist and your other hand holding it near the tip, pipe swirls of the frosting onto the cupcakes. Decorate with sprinkles and serve.

# Lemony Whoopie Pies

These yummy, colorful treats, which sandwich a sweet, fluffy filling between cake-like cookies, are ideal for sharing with friends on a summer afternoon. Make it your own and decorate with your favorite colorful cereal.

**1 PREPARE THE PANS.** Preheat the oven to 350°F. Line 2 cookie sheets with parchment paper.

**2 MAKE THE DOUGH.** In a medium bowl, mix the flour, baking soda, and salt. In a large bowl, using an electric mixer, beat together the butter and brown and granulated sugars on medium speed until light and fluffy, 2–3 minutes. Add the lemon zest and beat until well mixed, then add the egg and beat until incorporated. Reduce the speed to low, add half of the flour mixture, and beat just until combined. Add the buttermilk and vanilla and beat until combined. Add the remaining flour mixture and beat just until blended. Using a rubber spatula, gently fold in the sprinkles just until blended.

**3 BAKE THE COOKIES.** Using a small ice cream scoop, drop dough rounds onto the prepared pans, spacing them about 2 inches apart. Place 1 cookie sheet into the oven and bake the cookies until the tops are golden and firm to the touch, 9–10 minutes. Let cool on the pan on a wire rack for 5 minutes, then move the cookies directly to the rack and let cool completely, about 30 minutes. Repeat with the remaining cookie sheet of cookies.

**4 MAKE THE FILLING.** In a bowl, using an electric mixer, beat the butter on medium speed until light and fluffy, about 2 minutes. Reduce the speed to low, add the powdered sugar, milk, vanilla, lemon, and salt, and beat just until combined. Turn off the mixer and scrape down the sides of the bowl. Turn on the mixer to medium-high speed and beat until airy and smooth, about 5 minutes.

*Continue on next page*

## Makes 15 whoopie pies

FOR THE COOKIES

2 cups all-purpose flour

1½ teaspoons baking soda

½ teaspoon salt

6 tablespoons unsalted butter, at room temperature

½ cup firmly packed light brown sugar

½ cup granulated sugar

Grated zest of 1 lemon (about 1 tablespoon)

1 large egg

1 cup buttermilk

1 teaspoon pure vanilla extract

2 tablespoons nonpareil sprinkles

**5** **FILL THE COOKIES.** Turn half of the cookies bottom side up. You can make as many different colors of filling as you like. Divide the filling among as many small bowls as colors you are making. Add a few dabs of a single food coloring to each bowl. Using a spoon or rubber spatula, mix until the color is evenly blended. If needed, add more food coloring until you have the desired color. Scoop each color into its own lock-top plastic bag, twist the top closed, and cut off a corner. Pipe the filling onto the overturned cookies, using a single color on each cookie. Top each filled cookie with a second cookie, bottom side down, to create a cookie sandwich.

**6** **DIP THE COOKIES.** Fill a small bowl with the colorful cereal. Roll the edge of a cookie sandwich in the crushed cereal, coating the filling evenly with the cereal, then set aside on a serving plate. Repeat with the remaining cookies. Serve right away.

FOR THE FILLING

½ cup unsalted butter, at room temperature

2½ cups powdered sugar

3 tablespoons whole milk

½ teaspoon pure vanilla extract

½ teaspoon pure lemon extract

Pinch of salt

Selection of gel paste food coloring, such as pink, blue, purple, and/or yellow

1 cup colorful cereal of your choice

**HEALTHY TIP!**
Like a bite-size treat? This recipe can also make 30 mini whoopie pies. Use a teaspoon to drop dough rounds onto the cookie sheets and bake for 8 minutes.

# Morning Treats

# Baby Banana Breads

ASK FOR HELP!

You'll want to make sure you use very ripe bananas—look for lots of brown spots on the skin—so they're easy to mash and the breads will turn out moist and flavorful. If you don't want to make banana bread right away, you can freeze ripe bananas for up to 3 months and then thaw them when you're ready to bake.

*1* **PREPARE THE PANS.** Preheat the oven to 350°F. Butter three 5½ x 3-inch loaf pans or four 3½ x 2½-inch loaf pans, then dust with flour, tapping out the excess.

*2* **MAKE THE BATTER.** In a medium bowl, mix the flour, sugar, baking soda, and salt. Peel the bananas, drop them into a large bowl, and mash well with a fork. Add the butter, eggs, yogurt, and vanilla to the bananas and stir until well mixed. Gradually add the flour mixture, stirring gently just until mixed. Add the nuts, if using, and stir to distribute evenly. Scrape the batter into the prepared pans, dividing it evenly and smoothing the tops.

*3* **BAKE THE BREADS.** Bake the breads until a toothpick inserted into the center of each loaf comes out clean, about 40 minutes for the 5½ x 3-inch pans and about 30–35 minutes for the 3 ½ x 2 ½ pans. If the tops begin to brown too much before the breads are ready, cover them loosely with aluminum foil. Let cool in the pans on wire racks for 10 minutes, then turn the loaves out onto the racks, turn top side up, and let cool completely before serving.

## Makes 8–10 servings

½ cup unsalted butter, melted and cooled, plus room-temperature butter for the pans

2¼ cups all-purpose flour, plus more for the pans

1 cup sugar

1 teaspoon baking soda

½ teaspoon salt

3 very ripe bananas

2 large eggs, lightly beaten

⅓ cup plain yogurt

1 teaspoon pure vanilla extract

1 cup chopped walnuts (optional)

**HEALTHY TIP!**
Serve these alongside some fresh yogurt or your favorite nut butter!

# Carrot-Apple Muffins

ASK FOR HELP!

These muffins are so good you won't even know you're getting a serving of both a fruit and a vegetable! The Greek yogurt, which provides a boost of protein and calcium, makes them deliciously moist and a great option for a grab-and-go school snack.

*1* **PREPARE THE MUFFIN CUPS.** Preheat the oven to 400°F. Line 12 standard muffin cups with paper liners.

*2* **MAKE THE BATTER.** In a bowl, mix the all-purpose flour, whole wheat flour, oat bran, sugar, baking powder, baking soda, salt, cinnamon, and chia seeds. In a large bowl, using an electric mixer, beat the eggs on low speed until blended, then beat in the yogurt and butter until well mixed. Add the flour mixture and mix on low speed just until combined. The batter will be very thick and slightly dry. Using a rubber spatula or wooden spoon, mix in the apple and carrot just until evenly distributed. Do not overmix or the muffins will turn out tough.

*3* **BAKE THE MUFFINS.** Using a large ice cream scoop, fill each prepared muffin cup about three-fourths full. If using the topping, in a small bowl, stir together the turbinado sugar and cinnamon. Sprinkle the topping on the batter in each muffin cup, dividing it evenly. Bake the muffins until a toothpick inserted into the center of a muffin comes out clean, 16–18 minutes. Let cool in the pan on a wire rack for about 5 minutes, then carefully turn the muffins out onto the rack and let cool completely. Serve at room temperature.

## Makes 12 muffins

⅔ cup all-purpose flour

⅔ cup whole-wheat flour

¼ cup oat or wheat bran

½ cup firmly packed light brown sugar

1½ teaspoons baking powder

½ teaspoon baking soda

½ teaspoon salt

1 teaspoon ground cinnamon

2 tablespoons chia seeds

2 large eggs

1 cup plain whole-milk Greek yogurt

4 tablespoons unsalted butter, melted and cooled

1 cup peeled and grated tart apple, such as Granny Smith (about 1 large apple)

1 cup peeled and grated carrot (about 2 carrots)

FOR THE TOPPING (OPTIONAL)

2 tablespoons turbinado sugar

1 teaspoon ground cinnamon

# Walnut-Zucchini Bread

ASK FOR HELP!

The zucchini is what gives this bread the bulk of its tenderness and moisture, which reduces the need for a large amount of butter. If you don't like walnuts, you can always substitute pecans or almonds in their place.

*1* **PREPARE THE PAN(S).** Preheat the oven to 350°F. Line three 5½ x 3-inch loaf pans or one 9 x 5-inch loaf pan with parchment paper, cutting the short sides to fit the bottom and cutting the long sides to reach 2 inches up the sides of the pan.

*2* **BEGIN THE BATTER.** Using a box grater-shredder, shred the zucchini on the large holes. In a large bowl, using an electric mixer, beat together the sugar, oil, eggs, and vanilla on medium speed until pale and creamy, about 1 minute. Switch to a wooden spoon and stir in the zucchini until blended.

*3* **FINISH THE BATTER.** In a bowl, stir together the flour, baking powder, cinnamon, salt, baking soda, prunes, and walnuts. Add the flour mixture to the zucchini mixture and stir with the wooden spoon just until combined. The batter will be stiff. Scrape the batter into the prepared pan(s) and smooth the top(s).

*4* **BAKE THE BREAD.** Bake the bread until it is firm to the touch and pulls away from the pan sides, 35–40 minutes for the small loaves or 50–60 minutes for the large loaf. A toothpick inserted into the center of a loaf should come out clean. Let cool in the pan(s) on a wire rack for 10 minutes, then turn out onto the rack and let cool completely before serving.

**Makes 3 mini loaves
or 1 regular loaf**

½ lb zucchini, trimmed

¾ cup sugar

½ cup canola oil

2 large eggs

1 teaspoon pure vanilla extract

1½ cups all-purpose flour, plus more if needed

2 teaspoons baking powder

1½ teaspoons ground cinnamon

½ teaspoon salt

¼ teaspoon baking soda

½ cup pitted moist-pack prunes, chopped

⅓ cup walnuts, coarsely chopped

# Heart-Shaped Scones

Every day is a good day to tell someone you love them. That means these scones are not only wonderful for a Valentine's Day breakfast but are also a great anytime gift for the special people in your life. Plus, they're super easy to make.

**1** **MAKE THE DOUGH.** Preheat the oven to 425°F. In a large bowl, mix the flour, baking powder, sugar, and salt. Add the cherries and cream and stir just until combined. Using your hands, gently gather up the dough and knead it against the side of the bowl until it holds together in a rough ball.

**2** **ROLL OUT AND CUT THE DOUGH.** Turn out the dough onto a floured work surface. Using a rolling pin, roll out the dough until about ¾ inch thick. Using a 3-inch-wide heart-shaped cookie cutter, cut out as many hearts as possible. Move the cutouts to a rimmed baking sheet, spacing them at least 2 inches. Gather up the dough scraps, press them together, knead briefly, and roll out and cut out more hearts. You should have 10 scones total.

**3** **ADD THE TOPPING.** To make the topping, pour the cream into a small cup. Using a pastry brush, lightly brush the top of each heart with the cream, then sprinkle with the sugar, dividing it evenly.

**4** **BAKE THE SCONES.** Bake the scones until golden, 10–12 minutes. Transfer to a wire rack to cool. Serve warm or at room temperature.

## Makes 10 scones

2 cups all-purpose flour, plus more for dusting

1 tablespoon baking powder

2 teaspoons sugar

1 teaspoon salt

½ cup dried cherries, cranberries, or strawberries

¾ cup plus 2 tablespoons heavy cream

FOR THE TOPPING

1 tablespoon heavy cream

1 tablespoon sugar

# Classic Popovers

 ASK FOR HELP!

A popover is a type of light and airy roll with a hollow center. In the morning, you can fill that hollow with a favorite jam or finely diced fresh fruit. If you have any leftover popovers, they're great for soaking up soup or gravy at dinnertime.

1 **MAKE THE BATTER.** Preheat the oven to 450°F. In a bowl, mix the flour and salt. Make a well in the center of the flour mixture and add the milk and eggs to the well. Whisk the wet ingredients into the flour mixture just until combined.

2 **PREHEAT AND FILL THE PAN.** Place a 12-cup popover pan or standard muffin pan into the preheated oven and heat until hot, about 2 minutes. Remove from the oven and spoon 1 teaspoon of the melted butter into each cup. Divide the batter evenly among the cups, filling them half full.

3 **BAKE THE POPOVERS.** Bake the popovers for 10 minutes. Reduce the oven temperature to 375°F and continue to bake, without opening the oven door, until the popovers are puffed, crisp, and golden brown, 20–25 minutes longer. Remove the pan from the oven. Have an adult help you remove the piping-hot popovers from the pan. Serve right away with butter, if desired, and jam.

## Makes 12 popovers

1 cup all-purpose flour

½ teaspoon salt

1 cup whole milk

2 large eggs, at room temperature, lightly beaten

4 tablespoons unsalted butter, melted, plus room-temperature butter for serving (optional)

Jam of choice for serving

**HEALTHY TIP!**
No peeking! Opening the oven door while the popovers are still baking will cause them to collapse.

# Mini Blueberry Muffins

 ASK FOR HELP!

Here are easy-to-pack on-the-go treats that will energize you throughout the day, whatever you may be doing. Be careful not to overmix the batter or the muffins will bake up tough and chewy. The batter is just right when the flour is fully mixed in but lumps are still visible.

*1* **MAKE THE BATTER.** In a bowl, whisk together the eggs, brown sugar, oil, cream, milk, and vanilla. In a large bowl, sift together the flour, baking powder, nutmeg, and salt. Make a well in the center of the flour mixture and slowly pour in the egg mixture. Gradually mix the wet ingredients into the flour mixture just until combined. Add the butter and stir until almost smooth but still slightly lumpy. Do not overmix. The batter will be fairly thick. Using a rubber spatula, gently fold the blueberries into the batter just until evenly distributed.

*2* **BAKE THE MUFFINS.** Preheat the oven to 400°F. Butter 24 mini muffin cups. Spoon the batter into the prepared muffin cups, filling each cup three-fourths full. Bake the muffins until a toothpick inserted into the center of a muffin comes out clean, 12–14 minutes. Let cool in the pan on a wire rack for 5 minutes, then turn the muffins out onto the rack. Turn top side up and drizzle with the glaze, if using. Serve warm.

## Make 24 mini muffins

2 large eggs

½ cup firmly packed light brown sugar

⅓ cup canola oil

½ cup heavy cream

½ cup whole milk

1½ teaspoons pure vanilla extract

2¼ cups all-purpose flour

2 teaspoons baking powder

¼ teaspoon ground nutmeg

⅛ teaspoon salt

3 tablespoons unsalted butter, melted and cooled, plus room-temperature butter for the muffin cups

1½ cups fresh blueberries

Thick Vanilla Glaze (page 116), without food coloring (optional)

# Strawberry-Citrus Muffins

 ASK FOR HELP!

The strawberries, strawberry jam, and orange zest make these muffins a great late-spring morning treat, especially if you use strawberries bought at a farmers' market. Be sure you pat the strawberries dry before adding them to the batter or they will turn it streaky pink.

*1* **PREPARE THE MUFFIN CUPS.** Preheat the oven to 400°F. Line 16 standard muffin cups with paper liners; fill any unused cups in the pans one-third full with water.

*2* **MAKE THE BATTER.** In a large bowl, mix the flour, baking powder, baking soda, and salt. In a medium bowl, whisk together the sugar, milk, sour cream, oil, egg, and orange zest until well mixed and smooth. Add the strawberries and stir gently to mix. Pour the milk mixture into the flour mixture and stir just until blended. Do not overmix.

*3* **FILL THE MUFFIN CUPS.** Place a spoonful of batter into each prepared muffin cup. Add a scant 1 teaspoon strawberry jam to each cup, then spoon the remaining batter on top, filling each cup about two-thirds full.

*4* **BAKE THE MUFFINS.** Bake the muffins until a toothpick inserted into the center of a muffin comes out clean, 15–18 minutes. Let cool in the pans on wire racks for 5 minutes, then carefully turn the muffins out onto the racks. Turn top side up and drizzle with the glaze. Serve warm or at room temperature.

## Makes 16 muffins

2¼ cups all-purpose flour

2 teaspoons baking powder

1 teaspoon baking soda

½ teaspoon salt

¾ cup sugar

½ cup whole milk, at room temperature

½ cup sour cream, at room temperature

½ cup canola oil

1 large egg, at room temperature

1 tablespoon grated orange zest

1 cup hulled and thinly sliced fresh strawberries, patted dry

About ⅓ cup strawberry jam

Thick Vanilla Glaze (page 116)

**HEALTHY TIP!**
Try swapping out the glaze in favor of your favorite nut butter, fruit butter, or yogurt for a lighter morning snack.

# Spiced Pumpkin Bread

Back to school already? Spend a weekend baking this bread and you'll have a yummy treat for weekday mornings. This recipe makes two loaves, so you can keep one at room temperature for up to 4 days and wrap the other one tightly in plastic wrap and store it in the freezer for up to 6 months.

1. **PREPARE THE PANS.** Preheat the oven to 350°F. Butter two 9 x 5-inch loaf pans, then dust with flour, tapping out the excess. Set aside.

2. **MAKE THE BATTER.** In a medium bowl, mix the flour, baking soda, salt, baking powder, cinnamon, cloves, and nutmeg. In a large bowl, combine the pumpkin, sugar, oil, eggs, and vanilla and stir until well mixed. Gradually add the flour mixture to the pumpkin mixture, stirring just until blended. Scrape the batter into the prepared pans, dividing it evenly and smoothing the tops. Sprinkle the nuts evenly over the tops, if using.

3. **BAKE THE BREADS.** Bake the breads until the tops are lightly browned and a toothpick inserted into the center of each loaf comes out clean, 50–55 minutes. Let cool in the pans on wire racks for 10 minutes, then turn the loaves out onto the racks, turn top side up, and let cool completely.

4. **FINISH WITH THE GLAZE.** Move the loaves to serving plates and drizzle with the glaze, allowing it to run down the sides. Let stand for about 5 minutes to allow the glaze to set, then cut into slices to serve.

## Makes about 16 servings

Unsalted butter for the pans

3 cups all-purpose flour, plus more for dusting

1½ teaspoons baking soda

1½ teaspoons salt

1 teaspoon baking powder

1 teaspoon ground cinnamon

1 teaspoon ground cloves

1 teaspoon ground nutmeg

1 can (15 oz) pumpkin purée

3 cups sugar

1 cup canola oil

3 large eggs, at room temperature

1 teaspoon pure vanilla extract

½ cup chopped walnuts (optional)

Thick Vanilla Glaze (page 116), without food coloring

# Easy Monkey Bread

ASK FOR HELP!

This sticky-sweet and cinnamony monkey bread would be gone in a heartbeat if Barbie baked it for her friends and family. As the little balls of dough bake, they stick together, but they're easy to pull apart afterward, making it the perfect shareable snack.

1 **PREPARE THE PAN AND TOPPINGS.** Using a pastry brush, brush a 10-inch Bundt pan with some of the butter. Set aside the remaining butter in a small, shallow bowl. In another small, shallow bowl, stir together the sugar, ½ cup of the pecans, and the cinnamon and set aside. Sprinkle the remaining 2 tablespoons pecans over the bottom of the prepared pan.

2 **ASSEMBLE THE LOAF.** Put the thawed rolls on a floured work surface. Working with a few rolls at a time, roll them in the melted butter and then turn them in the sugar mixture to coat evenly. As the rolls are ready, arrange them in a roughly even layer in the prepared pan.

3 **LET IT RISE.** Preheat the oven to 350°F for 5 minutes, then turn off the oven. Cover the dough-filled pan loosely with aluminum foil and place it in the warm oven. Let the dough rise until doubled in bulk, about 1 hour. Remove the pan from the oven, then preheat the oven to 375°F.

4 **BAKE THE BREAD.** Bake the bread until richly browned and a toothpick inserted into the center of the loaf comes out clean, 30–35 minutes. Let cool in the pan on a wire rack for 5 minutes. Using oven mitts, hold a serving plate upside down on top of the pan, then turn the pan and plate over together, releasing the loaf onto the plate and lifting off the pan. Serve warm.

## Makes about 8 servings

½ cup unsalted butter, melted and cooled

1 cup firmly packed light brown sugar

½ cup plus 2 tablespoons finely chopped pecans

2½ teaspoons ground cinnamon

All-purpose flour for dusting

1 package (25 oz) frozen Parker House–style rolls, thawed

# Cherry Doughnuts with Pastel Confetti

No hot oil is needed here. Instead of frying the doughnuts, you bake them, which results in a fluffy pastry that still goes great with a glass of milk on a Saturday morning.

*1* **MAKE THE DOUGH.** In a bowl, sift together the flour, baking powder, and salt. In a large bowl, using an electric mixer, beat together the egg and sugar on low speed until creamy and pale. Add the milk, butter, and vanilla and almond extracts and beat until well blended. With the mixer still on low speed, add the flour mixture and beat just until a soft dough forms. Turn off the mixer. Add the cherries and stir with a wooden spoon until evenly distributed. Cover and refrigerate the dough until firm, at least 1 hour or up to overnight.

*2* **PREPARE THE PAN.** Preheat the oven to 400°F. Line 1 rimmed baking sheet with parchment paper and butter the paper.

*3* **CUT OUT THE DOUGHNUTS.** Turn out the dough onto a floured work surface. Dust a rolling pin with flour, then roll out the dough into a round about 10 inches in diameter and ½ inch thick. Using a 3-inch round pastry cutter, cut out as many rounds as possible. Then, using a 1-inch round pastry cutter, cut out a hole from the center of each round. Move the large cutouts to the prepared pan, spacing them about 1½ inches apart. Gather up the dough scraps and holes, press them together, roll out, and cut out more rounds and holes. You should have about 10 doughnuts. Add the holes from the second batch of cutouts to the pan.

*4* **BAKE AND GLAZE THE DOUGHNUTS.** Bake the doughnuts until the tops are lightly golden, about 20 minutes; the doughnut holes will be ready in about 15 minutes. Transfer to a wire rack and let cool for about 10 minutes. Put the glaze into a shallow bowl. One at a time, dip the top of each doughnut into the glaze, then return the doughnut, top side up, to the rack and decorate with sprinkles. Dip and decorate the doughnut holes the same way, if you like. Let stand until the glaze is set, about 10 minutes, before serving.

## Makes about 10 doughnuts

FOR THE DOUGH

2 cups all-purpose flour, plus more for dusting

1½ teaspoons baking powder

¼ teaspoon salt

1 large egg

½ cup sugar

½ cup whole milk

3 tablespoons unsalted butter, melted and cooled, plus room-temperature butter for the pan

1 teaspoon pure vanilla extract

¼ teaspoon pure almond extract

¾ cup dried cherries, finely chopped

Thick Vanilla Glaze (page 116), warmed just until pourable

Quin sprinkles for decorating

# BASICS

## Vanilla Cookie Icing

2 cups powdered sugar

2 tablespoons warm water

1 tablespoon light corn syrup

1 teaspoon pure vanilla extract

2–3 dabs gel paste food coloring of choice

**Makes 1 cup**

In a bowl, whisk together the sugar, water, corn syrup, and vanilla until smooth. Whisk in the food coloring until evenly mixed, starting with 2 dabs and adding more if you want a darker color. If the icing is too thick, whisk in more warm water, ½ teaspoon at a time, for the desired consistency.

## Thick Vanilla Glaze

6 tablespoons unsalted butter, melted

2½ cups powdered sugar

1 teaspoon pure vanilla extract

5 tablespoons hot water, plus more if needed

1–2 drops of red food coloring

**Makes about 3 cups**

In a bowl, whisk together the butter, sugar, vanilla, and hot water until smooth. Add the food coloring and stir to tint the glaze a pretty pink. If the glaze is too thick, whisk in more hot water, 1 teaspoon at a time, for the desired consistency. Use right away.

## Vanilla Cake Icing

2 cups powdered sugar, sifted

3 tablespoons whole milk, plus more if needed

1 teaspoon pure vanilla extract

2–3 drops of food coloring of choice

**Makes 1 cup**

In a bowl, stir together the sugar, milk, and vanilla until smooth. Add 2 drops of the food coloring and whisk to combine. Whisk in the remaining drop if you want a darker color.

## Whipped Cream

1½ cups heavy cream

¼ cup powdered sugar

½ teaspoon pure vanilla extract

**Makes about 2 cups**

In a bowl, using an electric mixer, beat together the cream, sugar, and vanilla on medium speed until light and fluffy, about 3 minutes.

## Sugar-Free Peanut Butter Chocolate Spread

½ cup creamy peanut butter

¼ cup cocoa powder

5 tablespoons nut or dairy milk

3 tablespoon maple syrup

**Makes about 1¼ cups**

In a bowl, combine the peanut butter, cocoa powder, milk, and maple syrup. Stir until evenly blended.

## Chocolate Frosting

3½ cups powdered sugar

1 cup unsweetened cocoa powder

½ cup unsalted butter, cut into 8 pieces,
at room temperature

1 teaspoon pure vanilla extract

Pinch of salt

1 cup heavy cream, plus more if needed

### Makes 3 cups

In a large bowl, stir together the sugar and cocoa. Add the
butter. Using an electric mixer, beat the mixture on low
speed just until crumbly. Add the vanilla and salt and beat
until combined. Turn off the mixer. Add the cream and
beat on medium speed for about 1 minute. The frosting
should be smooth and spreadable; if it is too thick, beat
in more cream, 1 teaspoon at a time, for the desired
consistency.

## Buttercream Frosting

1 cup unsalted butter, at room temperature

6 cups powdered sugar

1 tablespoon pure vanilla extract

¼ cup heavy cream

### Makes about 4 cups

In a bowl, using an electric mixer, beat the butter on
medium-high speed until light and fluffy, about 2 minutes.
Add the sugar in two batches, beating well after each
addition. Add the vanilla and beat until smooth, about
1 minute. Add the cream and beat until thick and creamy,
about 3 minutes.

## Double-Crust Flaky Pie Pastry

3 cups all-purpose flour

2 teaspoons sugar

1 teaspoon salt

1 cup very cold unsalted butter, cut into small cubes

½ cup ice-cold water, plus more if needed

### Makes dough for two 9-inch pies or 8 pie pops

In a bowl, mix the flour, sugar, and salt. Scatter the butter over
the flour mixture. Using a pastry blender, 2 knives, or your
fingertips, cut or rub in the butter until large, coarse crumbs
form. Sprinkle the water over the top and, using a fork, stir
and toss lightly until the dough begins to hold together in
large clumps. If the dough is too crumbly, mix in a little more
water, 1 teaspoon at a time. Dump the dough onto a work
surface and press into a mound. Divide the dough in half.
Wrap each half separately in plastic wrap and then press into
a thick disk. Refrigerate for at least 1 hour or up to 3 days.

## Sprinkle Cookie Frosting

½ cup unsalted butter, at cool room temperature

3 cups powdered sugar

2 tablespoons heavy cream, plus more if needed

1 teaspoon pure vanilla extract

Yellow, pink, or blue food coloring

### Makes about 4 cups

In a bowl, using an electric mixer, beat the butter on
medium-high until fluffy, 1 minute. With the mixer off, sift
half of the powdered sugar into the butter. Beat on low
for 1 minute. Sift the remaining powdered sugar into the
butter and beat on low until the mixture looks like bread
crumbs, 1 minute. Add the cream and vanilla, increase
the speed to medium-high, and beat until smooth and
creamy, 2 minutes. Add a few drops of food coloring and
continue to beat until the color is evenly blended.

# Convert it, Swap it, Halve it

## MEASUREMENT CONVERSIONS

3 teaspoons = 1 tablespoon

4 tablespoons = ¼ cup

5 tablespoons plus 1 teaspoon = ⅓ cup

1 cup = 8 fluid ounces

2 cups = 1 pint

2 pints = 1 quart

4 quarts = 1 gallon

4 ounces = ¼ pound

8 ounces = ½ pound

12 ounces = ¾ pound

16 ounces = 1 pound

## MISSING SOMETHING?

**Buttermilk**

For every 1 cup buttermilk needed, stir together 1 cup whole milk and 1 tablespoon fresh lemon juice or distilled white vinegar. Let the mixture sit for a few minutes, or until thickened and slightly curdled.

**Heavy Cream**

For every 1 cup heavy cream needed, stir together ¾ cup whole milk and ⅓ cup melted and cooled unsalted butter. This substitution will not work if the recipe calls for whipping the cream.

**Eggs**

For cake and quick bread batters, substitute ¼ cup applesauce or ½ mashed banana for every egg called for in the recipe. For cookies, brownies, and muffins, whisk together 1 tablespoon flaxseed meal and 2½ tablespoons water for every egg called for in the recipe. Let stand for 5 minutes, or until thickened, before using. This flaxseed "egg" will not thicken as much as a whisked regular egg.

# Index

Lemon Tartlets with Glittery Blossoms, page 55

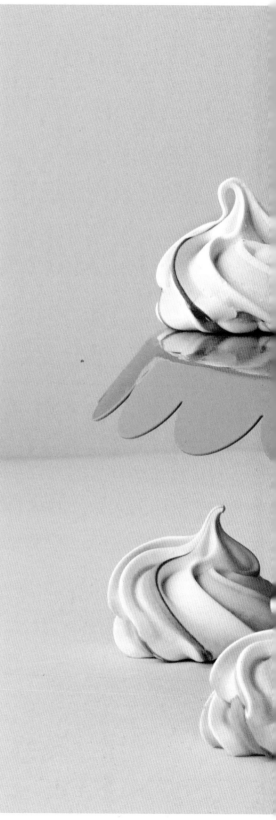

Yellow & Pink Swirly
Meringues,, page 37

# weldon**owen**

1150 Brickyard Cove Road
Richmond, CA 94801
www.weldonowen.com

WELDON OWEN INTERNATIONAL

CEO  Raoul Goff
Publisher  Roger Shaw
Associate Publisher  Amy Marr
Senior Editor  Lisa Atwood
Editorial Assistant  Jourdan Plautz
Creative Director  Chrissy Kwasnik
Art Director  Bronwyn Lane
Design Support  Megan Sinead Harris
Managing Editor  Tarji Rodriguez
Production Manager  Binh Au
Imaging Manager  Don Hill

Photographer  Ted Thomas
Food Stylist  Abby Stolfo
Prop Stylist  Kerrie Sherrell Walsh

Printed and bound in China

First printed in 2020
10 9 8 7 6 5 4 3 2

Library of Congress Cataloging in
Publication data is available

ISBN: 978-1-68188-517-9

ACKNOWLEDGMENTS

Weldon Owen wishes to thank the following people for their generous help in the production of this book:
Kim Laidlaw, Veronica Laramie, Elizabeth Parsons, and Sharon Silva.